Keep it Simple. Make it Special.

SLOW COOKER
to the Rescue

Dedication

For every cook who needs an extra helping hand in the kitchen!

Appreciation

To all our Gooseberry Patch friends who have shared their favorite slow cooker recipes with us...thank you!

Gooseberry Patch
An imprint of Globe Pequot
246 Goose Lane • Guilford, CT 06437

www.gooseberrypatch.com
1•800•854•6673

U.S. to Metric Recipe Equivalents

Volume Measurements

1/4 teaspoon	1 mL
1/2 teaspoon	2 mL
1 teaspoon	5 mL
1 tablespoon = 3 teaspoons	15 mL
2 tablespoons = 1 fluid ounce	30 mL
1/4 cup	60 mL
1/3 cup	75 mL
1/2 cup = 4 fluid ounces	125 mL
1 cup = 8 fluid ounces	250 mL
2 cups = 1 pint =16 fluid ounces	500 mL
4 cups = 1 quart	1 L

Weights

1 ounce	30 g
4 ounces	120 g
8 ounces	225 g
16 ounces = 1 pound	450 g

Oven Temperatures

300° F	150° C
325° F	160° C
350° F	180° C
375° F	190° C
400° F	200° C
450° F	230° C

Baking Pan Sizes

Square

8x8x2 inches	2 L = 20x20x5 cm
9x9x2 inches	2.5 L = 23x23x5 cm

Rectangular

13x9x2 inches	3.5 L = 33x23x5 cm

Loaf

9x5x3 inches	2 L = 23x13x7 cm

Round

8x1-1/2 inches	1.2 L = 20x4 cm
9x1-1/2 inches	1.5 L = 23x4 cm

Recipe Abbreviations

t. = teaspoon	ltr. = liter
T. = tablespoon	oz. = ounce
c. = cup	lb. = pound
pt. = pint	doz. = dozen
qt. = quart	pkg. = package
gal. = gallon	env. = envelope

Kitchen Measurements

A pinch = 1/8 tablespoon	1 fluid ounce = 2 tablespoons
3 teaspoons = 1 tablespoon	4 fluid ounces = 1/2 cup
2 tablespoons = 1/8 cup	8 fluid ounces = 1 cup
4 tablespoons = 1/4 cup	16 fluid ounces = 1 pint
8 tablespoons = 1/2 cup	32 fluid ounces = 1 quart
16 tablespoons = 1 cup	16 ounces net weight = 1 pound
2 cups = 1 pint	
4 cups = 1 quart	
4 quarts = 1 gallon	

Table of Contents

Hot Buffalo Dip

Hot Buffalo Dip

Vickie

3 to 4 boneless,
   skinless chicken
   breasts, cooked and
   chopped
2 8-oz. pkgs. cream
   cheese, cubed and
   softened

1 c. hot wing sauce
1/2 c. shredded
   Cheddar cheese
1/4 c. blue cheese salad
   dressing
corn chips, celery stalks

In a slow cooker, mix together all ingredients except
corn chips and celery stalks. Cover and cook on low
setting for 3 to 4 hours. Serve with corn chips and
celery stalks for dipping. Makes 8 to 10 servings.

South-of-the-Border Dip

Tonya Lewis, Crothersville, IN

1 lb. ground beef
1 lb. ground pork
   sausage
16-oz. pkg. Mexican
   pasteurized process
   cheese spread, cubed

10-3/4 oz. can cream of
   mushroom soup
4-oz. can chopped
   green chiles
tortilla chips

Brown ground beef and sausage in a skillet; drain.
Combine with cheese, soup and chiles in a slow cooker.
Cover and cook on low setting for 3 to 4 hours, until
cheese is melted. Serve with tortilla chips. Makes 7 to
8 cups.

Hot Broccoli-Cheese Dip

Rogene Rogers, Bemidji, MN

3/4 c. butter
3 stalks celery, thinly sliced
1 onion, chopped
4-oz. can sliced mushrooms, drained

3 T. all-purpose flour
10-3/4 oz. can cream of celery soup
3 c. shredded Cheddar cheese

10-oz. pkg. frozen chopped broccoli, thawed

Melt butter in a skillet over medium heat; sauté celery, onion and mushrooms. Stir in flour; mix well. Transfer mixture to a lightly greased slow cooker; mix in remaining ingredients. Cover and cook on high setting until cheese is melted, stirring every 15 minutes. Continue cooking, covered, on low setting for 2 to 4 hours. Makes 10 to 12 servings.

Hot Broccoli-Cheese Dip

Quick side

Creamy hot dips are twice as tasty with homemade baguette crisps! Thinly slice a French loaf and arrange slices on a baking sheet. Sprinkle with olive oil and garlic powder, then bake at 400 degrees for 12 to 15 minutes.

Creamy Hot Corn Dip

Tanya Miller, Millersburg, OH

2 8-oz. pkgs. cream cheese,
  softened
2 15-1/4 oz. cans corn, drained

1/2 c. butter
2 jalapeño peppers, diced
tortilla chips

Combine all ingredients except tortilla chips in a slow cooker. Cover and cook on high setting for 30 minutes; stir until smooth. Reduce setting to low to keep warm. The longer it cooks, the spicier it will get. Serve with tortilla chips. Makes 15 servings.

Honey-Garlic Meatballs

Candace Eshkakogan, Ontario, Canada

2 lbs. lean ground beef
2 eggs, beaten
4 to 5 saltine crackers, finely
  crushed

salt and pepper to taste
1 T. garlic powder
2 to 3 7.4-oz. jars honey-garlic
  barbecue sauce

In a large bowl, combine beef, eggs, crackers, salt, pepper and garlic powder; mix well. Roll beef mixture into one to 2-inch balls. Brown meatballs on all sides in a skillet over medium heat. Transfer meatballs to a slow cooker. Spoon barbecue sauce over meatballs. Cover and cook on high setting for 2 hours, or until meatballs are no long pink in the center. Serves 6 to 8.

Creamy Hot Corn Dip

Italian Scallion Meatballs

Italian Scallion Meatballs

Wendy Jacobs, Idaho Falls, ID

1 c. grape juice
1 c. apple jelly
1 c. catsup
8-oz. can tomato sauce
4 lbs. frozen Italian-style meatballs
Garnish: sliced green onions

In a small saucepan, combine all ingredients except meatballs. Cook and stir over medium heat until jelly is melted; remove from heat. Place meatballs in a slow cooker; pour sauce over top and gently stir to coat. Cover and cook on low setting for 4 hours. Sprinkle with onions at serving time. Makes about 11 dozen.

Pizza Fondue

Shannon Finewood, Corpus Christi, TX

28-oz. jar spaghetti sauce
16-oz. pkg. shredded mozzarella cheese
1/4 c. grated Parmesan cheese
2 T. dried oregano
2 T. dried parsley
1 T. garlic powder
1 t. dried, minced onion
Italian bread cubes, pepperoni chunks, whole mushrooms, green pepper slices

Combine sauce, cheeses and seasonings in a slow cooker; mix well. Cover and cook on low setting for 2 hours, or until warmed through and cheese is melted; stir. Serve with desired dippers. Makes 10 servings.

Texas Queso Dip

Amy Shilliday, San Antonio, TX

1 lb. hot ground pork sausage, browned and drained
2 lbs. pasteurized process cheese spread, cubed
10-oz. can diced tomatoes with green chiles
1/2 c. milk
white corn tortilla chips

Combine all ingredients except tortilla chips in a slow cooker. Cover and cook on low setting until cheese is melted, about 2 hours. Serve with tortilla chips. Makes 10 to 12 servings.

Quick tip

Keep a pair of kitchen shears handy. They make short work of snipping herbs, dicing bacon or even cutting cheese slices into shreds.

Chipotle-Black Bean Dip

Vickie

16-oz. can refried beans
15-oz. can black beans, drained and rinsed
11-oz. can sweet corn & diced peppers, drained

1 c. chunky salsa
2 chipotle chiles in adobo sauce, chopped and 2 t. adobo sauce reserved

1-1/2 c. shredded Cheddar cheese
4 green onions, chopped
tortilla chips

Mix together beans, corn, salsa, chiles, reserved adobo sauce and one cup cheese in a slow cooker. Cover and cook on low setting for 3 to 4 hours, stirring after 2 hours. Sprinkle with remaining cheese and onions. Keep warm on low setting; serve with tortilla chips. Makes 12 servings.

Slow-Cooker Spinach & Artichoke Dip

Angie Ellefson, Milton, WI

10-oz. pkg. frozen chopped spinach, thawed and drained
13-oz. can artichoke hearts, drained and chopped
7-oz. pkg. shredded mozzarella and Asiago cheese blend with roasted garlic

6-oz. pkg. shredded Asiago and Parmesan cheese blend
8-oz. pkg. low-fat cream cheese cubed
1 c. light sour cream
1 c. light mayonnaise

3 T. garlic, minced
white pepper to taste
1/4 to 1/3 c. milk
assorted dippers, such as toasted baguette slices and corn chips

Combine all ingredients except milk and dippers in a slow cooker. Cover and cook on high setting for 2 hours, or until cheese is melted. Stir in milk until desired dipping consistency is reached. Turn slow cooker to low setting. Serve with assorted dippers. Makes 8 to 10 servings.

Quick tip

A party buffet looks oh-so inviting when risers are used to raise up serving bowls and baskets. Arrange upside-down cake pans or shallow dishes and drape with a tablecloth, then set food containers on top!

Chipotle-Black Bean Dip

Roasted Cajun Pecans

Roasted Cajun Pecans

Becky Butler, Keller, TX

1 t. chili powder	1/2 t. onion powder
1 t. dried basil	1/2 t. garlic powder
1 t. dried oregano	1/4 t. cayenne pepper
1 t. dried thyme	1/4 c. butter, melted
1 t. salt	1 lb. pecan halves

In a small bowl, mix together spices. Pour melted butter into a slow cooker; stir in pecans until evenly coated. Sprinkle spice mixture over pecans, stirring constantly, until evenly seasoned. Cover and cook on high setting for 12 to 15 minutes, stirring once. Remove lid from slow cooker and reduce heat to low setting. Cook, uncovered, for 2 hours, stirring occasionally. Remove pecans from slow cooker; cool on a paper towel-lined wire rack. Makes 8 servings.

Smoky-Good Snack Mix

Joshua Logan, Victoria, TX

4 c. bite-size crispy corn cereal squares	1/2 c. butter, melted
3 c. roasted whole almonds	2 T. smoke-flavored cooking sauce
10-oz. pkg. oyster crackers	1 T. Worcestershire sauce
9-oz. pkg. baked cheese snack crackers	1 t. seasoned salt

In a large slow cooker, combine cereal, almonds and crackers; set aside. In a small bowl, stir together remaining ingredients. Drizzle butter mixture over cereal mixture; toss to coat. Cook, uncovered, on high setting for 2-1/2 hours, stirring every 30 minutes. Cool completely; store in an airtight container. Makes about 17 cups.

Firecracker Party Mix

Darrell Lawry, Kissimmee, FL

8 c. popped popcorn	1/4 c. butter, melted
4 c. bite-size crispy corn cereal squares	2 T. brown sugar
3 c. pretzel sticks	1-1/2 t. salt
1/4 c. Worcestershire sauce	1/2 t. cayenne pepper

Combine popcorn, cereal and pretzels in a slow cooker; set aside. In a bowl, mix together sauce, butter, brown sugar, salt and pepper. Drizzle sauce mixture over popcorn mixture, stirring well to coat evenly. Cover and cook on low setting for 2 to 3 hours. Remove lid and cook on low setting for one more hour. Spoon party mixture onto a baking sheet to cool. Serve, or store in an airtight container. Will keep for about one week. Makes about 15 cups.

Bacon Dog Roll-Ups
Diana Chaney, Olathe, KS

1 lb. bacon, cut into thirds
2 1-lb. pkgs. mini cocktail
  wieners

1/2 to 3/4 c. brown sugar, packed

Wrap bacon slices around wieners; secure with toothpicks. Arrange one layer of wrapped wieners in bottom of slow cooker; sprinkle generously with brown sugar. Repeat layering, ending with more brown sugar. Cover and cook on low setting for 5 to 6 hours, or on high setting for 3 to 4 hours. Makes about 5 dozen.

BBQ Mustard Pigs
Beckie Apple, Grannis, AR

1 lb. mini smoked sausages
1/4 c. spicy brown mustard
2 c. barbecue sauce

1 c. grape jelly
1 T. smoke-flavored cooking sauce

Combine all ingredients in a slow cooker. Cover and cook on high setting for one to 2 hours, until sausages are heated through and sauce is thickened. Serves 6.

Glazed Kielbasa Bites
Janice Dorsey, San Antonio, TX

1 lb. Kielbasa, sliced
1 c. apricot preserves

1/2 c. maple syrup
2 T. bourbon or apple juice

Combine all ingredients in a slow cooker. Cover and cook on low setting for 4 hours. Serves 8 to 10.

Bacon Dog Roll-Ups

🥄🍴🔪 *Quick tip*

Make it easy for guests to mingle and chat...set up food at several tables instead of one big party buffet. Place hot foods on one table, chilled foods at another, sweets at yet another.

Apricot Brie Dip

Quick tip

Want to change the cooking time of a slow cooker recipe? It's simple...one hour of cooking on high equals 2 to 2-1/2 hours on low.

Tuscan White Bean Spread

Marlene Darnell, Newport Beach, CA

4 15-oz. cans cannellini beans,
  drained and rinsed
1 onion, chopped
4 cloves garlic, chopped
2 T. extra-virgin olive oil

1 c. water
1 t. dried rosemary
1 t. red pepper flakes
1 t. salt

1 t. pepper
crostini slices

Combine all ingredients except crostini in a slow cooker; stir. Cover and cook on high setting for 3 hours, or on low setting for 5 hours. Serve warm with crostini. Makes 10 to 12 servings.

Apricot Brie Dip

Emma Brown, Saskatchewan, Canada

1/2 c. dried apricots, finely
  chopped
1/4 c. apricot nectar or apple juice
1/3 c. plus 1 T. apricot preserves,
  divided

2-lb. Brie cheese round, rind
  removed and cubed
bread slices or crackers, cut-up
  vegetables

Combine apricots, nectar or juice and 1/3 cup preserves in a slow cooker. Cover and cook on high setting for 30 to 40 minutes, until hot. Stir in cheese. Cover and cook on high setting for an additional 30 to 40 minutes, until cheese is melted. Stir in remaining preserves. Turn slow cooker to low setting for serving. Serve with bread or crackers and vegetables for dipping. Serves 12.

Family Favorite Party Mix

Courtney Robinson, Columbus, OH

1 c. bite-size crispy wheat cereal
  squares
1 c. bite-size crispy rice cereal
  squares
1 c. bite-size crispy corn cereal
  squares

1 c. peanuts
1 c. pretzel sticks
1/4 c. butter, melted
2 T. Worcestershire sauce
1 t. seasoned salt

1 t. garlic salt
1 c. candy-coated chocolates
1 c. raisins

Combine cereals, nuts and pretzels in a slow cooker. Mix together butter, sauce and salts; gently stir into cereal mixture. Cover and cook on low setting for 3 to 4 hours. Uncover and cook on low setting for an additional 30 minutes; stir occasionally. Drain on paper towel-lined baking sheets; transfer to a large bowl. Cool. Add chocolates and raisins; toss to mix. Store in an airtight container. Makes 7 cups.

Ginger Thai Wings

Regina Vining, Warwick, RI

2-1/4 lbs. chicken wings
3/4 c. water, divided
1 T. lime juice
3/4 t. ground ginger, divided
1/2 c. creamy peanut butter
2 T. soy sauce
2 cloves garlic, minced
1/4 t. red pepper flakes

Place wings in a slow cooker. Add 1/4 cup water, lime juice and 1/4 teaspoon ginger to wings; stir to coat well. Cover and cook on low setting for 5 to 6 hours. Meanwhile, whisk together peanut butter, remaining water, remaining ginger and other ingredients in a small saucepan over medium heat. Cook, whisking constantly, until mixture is smooth. Remove wings to a serving bowl. Drizzle peanut sauce over wings. Toss to coat well. Serves 12.

Too-Easy Teriyaki Wings

Dwight Rutan, Clinton, OH

3/4 c. sugar
1/2 c. brown sugar, packed
1 t. garlic powder
1 t. ground ginger
1 c. soy sauce
3/4 c. water
1/4 c. pineapple juice
1/4 c. oil
4 lbs. chicken wings
Garnish: chopped green onion, sesame seed

In a large bowl, mix together all ingredients except wings. Add wings; toss to coat evenly. Cover and refrigerate at least 2 hours. Remove wings from marinade; place in a slow cooker. Pour one cup marinade over wings; discard remaining marinade. Cover and cook on low setting for 8 to 9 hours. Garnish with green onions and sesame seed before serving. Serves 4 to 6.

Chicken Wing Dip

Terri Scungio, Williamsburg, VA

1 lb. boneless, skinless chicken breasts, cooked and shredded
1 c. cayenne hot pepper sauce
1 c. blue cheese salad dressing
8-oz. pkg. cream cheese, softened
1 c. shredded mozzarella cheese
carrot and celery sticks, crackers

In a bowl, mix together shredded chicken and hot sauce; set aside. In a separate bowl, mix together salad dressing and cream cheese. Stir in mozzarella cheese and shredded chicken mixture. Transfer mixture to a mini slow cooker. Cover and cook on low setting for 2-1/2 to 3 hours, until heated through and cheese is melted. Serve with carrot and celery sticks and crackers. Serves 6 to 8.

Too-Easy Teriyaki Wings

Tipsy Dogs

Tipsy Dogs

Shirley McGlin, Black Creek, WI

2 1-lb. pkgs. mini
  cocktail wieners
2 c. catsup
3/4 c. brown sugar,
  packed
1 T. mustard

1/4 c. vinegar
1 onion, chopped
1/2 c. beer
Optional: hot pepper
  sauce

Combine all ingredients in a slow cooker. Cover and cook on low setting for 30 minutes to one hour, until hot. Serves 18 to 20.

Aunt Becky's Smoky Sausages

Sandra Smit, Arleta, CA

14-oz. pkg. mini smoked
  sausages
28-oz. bottle barbecue
  sauce
1-1/4 c. water

3 T. Worcestershire
  sauce
2 T. steak sauce
1/2 t. pepper

Combine all ingredients in a slow cooker; mix well. Cover and cook on low setting for 6 to 8 hours. Makes 8 servings.

Cranberry Kielbasa Bites

Kelley Annis, Massena, NY

2 16-oz. Kielbasa
  sausage rings, cut into
  1/2-inch pieces
2 14-oz. pkgs. mini
  smoked sausages

3/4 c. catsup
14-oz. can whole-berry
  cranberry sauce
1/2 c. grape jelly

Place all ingredients in a slow cooker; stir to mix well. Cover and cook on low setting for 7 to 8 hours. Serves 10 to 12.

Quick tip

Serving sticky finger foods? Fill a mini slow cooker set on low with rolled-up, dampened fingertip towels…guests will appreciate your thoughtfulness!

Kathy's Dilly Meatballs

Jennifer Heinl, Pittsburgh, PA

3 lbs. ground beef
1-1/2 c. dry bread
  crumbs
3/4 c. milk
3 eggs, beaten
1 onion, finely chopped
1 T. salt
1/4 t. pepper

1-1/2 t. Worcestershire
  sauce
3 10-3/4 oz. cans cream
  of chicken soup
1 c. milk
1 t. dill weed
1-1/2 c. sour cream
Garnish: fresh parsley,
  snipped

Combine first 8 ingredients in a large bowl. Form into one-inch balls; arrange on an ungreased 15"x10" jelly-roll pan. Bake at 350 degrees for 25 to 30 minutes, until lightly browned; drain and set aside. Combine soup, milk and dill in a slow cooker; add meatballs. Cover and cook on high setting until boiling, about 30 minutes, stirring occasionally. Reduce to low setting; cover and cook for one hour. Stir in sour cream; heat through. Sprinkle with parsley. Serves 15 to 20.

Quick tip

To make clean-up a breeze, lightly spray the inside of a slow cooker with non-stick vegetable spray before adding recipe ingredients. What a time-saver!

Swedish Meatballs

Jody Thiel, Ripon, WI

1 lb. ground beef
1 onion, chopped
6 graham crackers, finely
  crushed
1 T. sugar

1 t. salt
1/2 t. pepper
3 to 4 t. milk
10-1/2 oz. can beef broth

Combine all ingredients except broth in a large bowl. Mix well, adding a little extra milk if mixture appears too dry. Form into one-inch balls. Cook meatballs in a lightly greased skillet over medium heat until lightly browned, turning frequently. Remove meatballs from skillet; arrange in a slow cooker and set aside. Add broth to drippings in skillet; cook and stir over medium heat until slightly thickened. Pour broth mixture over meatballs; cover and cook on high setting for one hour. Serves 6.

Bob's Sweet-and-Sour Meatballs

Janet Owen, Vacaville, CA

1-1/2 lbs. ground beef
1 c. dry bread crumbs
1/3 c. onion, finely
  chopped
1 egg, beaten
1-1/2 t. salt
1/4 t. ground ginger
1/4 c. milk

20-oz. can pineapple
  chunks, drained and
  juice reserved
1/3 c. vinegar
1 T. soy sauce
1/2 c. brown sugar,
  packed
2 T. cornstarch

In a bowl, combine beef, bread crumbs, onion, egg, seasonings and milk. Shape into walnut-sized balls. Brown meatballs on all sides in a skillet over medium heat. Remove meatballs from skillet. Drain skillet; add reserved juice and remaining ingredients. Over medium heat, bring to a boil; boil for one minute. Add meatballs and pineapple chunks; simmer until meatballs are cooked through. For serving, transfer to a slow cooker; keep warm on low setting. Serves 8 to 10.

Swedish Meatballs

Slow-Cooker Buffalo Nachos

Slow-Cooker Buffalo Chicken Nachos

Rachel Hodges, Omaha, AR

1 lb. boneless, skinless chicken
  breasts
garlic salt to taste
salt and pepper to taste
12-oz. bottle buffalo wing sauce

1/2 c. ranch salad dressing
1/2 lb. pasteurized process cheese
  spread, cubed
10-oz. can diced tomatoes
  with green chiles

12-oz. pkg. tortilla chips

Place chicken in a slow cooker; sprinkle with garlic salt, salt and pepper. Pour in enough buffalo wing sauce to cover chicken. Cover and cook on low setting until very tender, about 4 hours. Shred chicken with 2 forks and drain off any excess liquid. Stir in salad dressing. In a saucepan, combine cheese and tomatoes with green chiles. Cook and stir until cheese melts. Layer tortilla chips on a large serving plate. Spoon cheese sauce over chips; top with chicken. Serves 6 to 8.

Quick & Easy Queso Blanco

Rita Morgan, Pueblo, CO

1 T. oil
1 onion, diced
1-1/2 t. garlic, minced
14-1/2 oz. can diced fire-roasted
  tomatoes, drained

4-1/2 oz. can chopped green chiles
1 c. milk
1-1/2 t. Mexican seasoning
1/2 t. coarse pepper

2 lbs. white American cheese,
  cubed
tortilla chips

Heat oil in a skillet over medium heat. Sauté onion and garlic in oil until onion is translucent, about 5 minutes. Combine onion mixture, tomatoes, chiles with juice, milk and seasonings in a slow cooker; stir to combine. Stir in cheese until well mixed. Cover and cook on low setting for 2 hours, or until cheese is melted and hot. Stir before serving. Serve with chips for dipping. Makes about 6 cups.

Chili Chicken Wings

Jason Keller, Carrollton, GA

4 lbs. chicken wings
12-oz. bottle chili sauce
3 to 4 T. hot pepper sauce

Arrange wings on a broiler pan. Broil 4 to 5 inches from heat until golden, about 10 minutes, turning to cook evenly. Transfer wings to a slow cooker. Combine sauces and pour over wings. Cover and cook on low setting for 4 to 5 hours, or on high setting for 2 to 2-1/2 hours. Serve with Blue Cheese Dip. Makes 3 to 4 dozen.

Blue Cheese Dip

3/4 c. mayonnaise
1/2 c. sour cream
1/2 c. crumbled blue
  cheese
2 T. fresh parsley,
  minced

1 T. lemon juice
1 T. white vinegar
1 clove garlic, minced
salt and pepper

Combine all ingredients; chill for one to 2 hours.

Texas Two-Step Dip

Tori Willis, Champaign, IL

1/2 lb. ground Italian
  pork sausage
1 onion, finely chopped
2 15-oz. cans refried
  beans
1-1/2 c. shredded
  Monterey Jack cheese

1-1/2 c. salsa
4-oz. can diced green
  chiles
1 t. ground cumin
corn chips or tortilla
  chips

Brown sausage and onion in a skillet over medium heat; drain. Spoon sausage mixture into a slow cooker. Stir in refried beans, cheese, salsa, green chiles with juice and cumin. Cover and cook on low setting, stirring occasionally, for 3 to 4 hours, until cheese is melted and dip is warmed through. Serve with chips for dipping. Serves 10 to 12.

Quick side

Make your own "baked" tortilla chips...it's easy. Spritz both sides of corn tortillas with non-stick cooking spray. Cut into wedges and microwave on high setting for 5 to 6 minutes, turning wedges over every 1-1/2 minutes. Sprinkle warm chips with sea salt and serve.

Chili Chicken Wings

Hawaiian Kielbasa

Quick tip

A paste made of equal parts cream of tartar and vinegar is a great mixture for removing stains on a slow cooker. Just rub on, then rinse well.

Hawaiian Kielbasa

Aemelia Manier, West Branch, MI

3 lbs. Kielbasa, sliced into 2-inch chunks
15-1/4 oz. can crushed pineapple
18-oz. bottle barbecue sauce
1/2 c. brown sugar, packed
1 T. ground ginger
1 t. onion powder
1 t. garlic powder

Combine all ingredients in a slow cooker. Mix well. Cover and cook on low setting for about 2 hours, until warmed through, or on high setting for about 30 minutes. Makes 10 to 15 servings.

Hot Brats

Barbara Imler, Noblesville, IN

2 to 2-1/2 lbs. bratwurst, knockwurst or Polish pork sausage, cut into 1-inch pieces
2 T. oil
12-oz. can regular or non-alcoholic beer
1/3 c. brown sugar, packed
2 T. cornstarch
1/3 c. vinegar
1/4 c. prepared horseradish
1/4 c. mustard

In a large skillet over medium-high heat, brown sausage in oil. Drain; add beer to skillet. Cover and simmer for 10 minutes. Meanwhile, in a small bowl, combine brown sugar and cornstarch; blend in vinegar, horseradish and mustard. Add mixture to sausages. Cover and cook until thickened and bubbly, stirring frequently. To serve, transfer to a slow cooker on low setting. Makes about 8 servings.

Saucy Kielbasa

Catherine Abbott, East Providence, RI

2 lbs. Kielbasa sausage
2 8-oz. jars Dijon mustard
3 10-oz. jars currant jelly

Cover Kielbasa with water in a medium saucepan; bring to a boil over medium-high heat. Simmer for 15 to 20 minutes; drain and cut into bite-size pieces. Combine all ingredients in a slow cooker. Cover and cook on low setting for one to 2 hours, until heated through. Serves 18 to 20.

Honey-Garlic Chicken Wings

Jennie Gist, Gooseberry Patch

3 lbs. chicken wings
salt and pepper to taste
1 c. honey
1/2 c. soy sauce
2 T. catsup
2 T. oil
1 clove garlic, minced

Sprinkle chicken wings with salt and pepper; place in a slow cooker and set aside. In a mixing bowl, combine remaining ingredients and mix well. Pour sauce over wings. Cover and cook on low setting for 6 to 8 hours. Makes 8 to 12 servings.

Plum Good Sausages & Meatballs

Athena Colegrove, Big Springs, TX

18-oz. bottle barbecue sauce
12-oz. jar plum preserves
16-oz. pkg. frozen meatballs
14-oz. pkg. mini smoked sausages

Combine sauce and preserves in a slow cooker; stir well. Add meatballs and sausages, stirring to coat. Cover and cook on low setting for 5 to 6 hours, or on high setting for 2-1/2 to 3 hours. Serve with toothpicks. Makes 12 servings.

Fiesta Taco Dip

Karen Hough, Knoxville, TN

16-oz. pkg. pasteurized processed cheese spread, cubed
2 8-oz. pkgs. cream cheese, softened
16-oz. jar salsa
1-1/4 oz. pkg. taco seasoning mix
1 lb. ground beef, browned and drained
corn or tortilla chips

Combine all ingredients except chips in a slow cooker. Cover and cook on low setting until cheeses melt, about one to 1-1/2 hours, stirring frequently. Serve with chips for dipping. Makes about 3-1/2 cups.

Plum Good Sausages & Meatballs

Seaside Crab Dip

Seaside Crab Dip

Lisa Columbo, Appleton, WI

2 8-oz. pkgs. cream cheese,
  softened
3 T. butter
1 bunch green onions, chopped

1 lb. crabmeat, flaked
onion and garlic salt to taste
garlic Melba toast

In a microwave-safe bowl, mix together all ingredients except Melba toast. Microwave on high setting until warm. Pour into a slow cooker; cover and keep warm on low setting. Serve with Melba toast. Makes 24 servings.

Spinach Queso Dip

Jessica Kraus, Delaware, OH

1 lb. Mexican-style pasteurized
  process cheese spread, cubed
10-oz. pkg. frozen chopped
  spinach, thawed and drained
  well

16-oz. container salsa
8-oz. pkg. cream cheese, cubed
Optional: chopped fresh cilantro
tortilla chips

Combine all ingredients except cilantro and tortilla chips in a slow cooker. Cover and cook on high setting for one to 2 hours, stirring occasionally, until cheeses are melted. Turn heat to low setting to keep warm. Stir in cilantro just before serving; serve with chips for dipping. Serves 10.

Creamy Seafood Dip

Lynda Robson, Boston, MA

2 10-3/4 oz. cans cream of celery
  soup
2 c. sharp pasteurized process
  cheese, grated
8-oz. pkg. crabmeat, flaked

1/2 c. cooked lobster, diced
1/2 c. cooked shrimp, chopped
1/8 t. paprika
1/8 t. nutmeg

1/8 t. cayenne pepper
1 loaf crusty bread, cut into
  1-inch cubes

Combine all ingredients except bread; stir well. Cover and cook on low setting for 2 hours, or until cheese is melted. Serve with bread cubes for dipping. Makes 6 to 7 cups.

Italian Mushrooms

Thomas Campbell, Eden Prairie, MN

4 lbs. small whole mushrooms, trimmed
2 c. butter, cut into thirds
0.7-oz. pkg. regular or zesty Italian salad dressing mix

Place mushrooms in a slow cooker; top with butter and seasoning mix. Cover and cook on high setting for 3 to 4 hours, stirring occasionally. Turn slow cooker to low setting to keep mushrooms warm. Serve with toothpicks. Makes 8 to 10 servings.

World's Best Cocktail Meatballs

Gina LiVolsi Norton, Wonder Lake, IL

1 lb. ground beef chuck
1/2 c. corn flake cereal, crushed
1/2 c. evaporated milk
12-oz. bottle chili sauce, divided
1 T. Worcestershire sauce
1/4 c. onion, finely chopped
1 t. salt
10-oz. jar grape jelly

In a bowl, combine beef, cereal, milk, 1/4 cup chili sauce, Worcestershire sauce, onion and salt; mix well. Cover and refrigerate for 30 minutes. Form beef mixture into walnut-size balls. Place meatballs on a baking sheet; bake at 375 degrees for 20 minutes, or until browned. Transfer meatballs to a slow cooker; set aside. In a saucepan over medium heat, combine remaining chili sauce and grape jelly. Cook and stir until jelly is melted; spoon over meatballs and stir gently. Set slow cooker to low setting for serving; heat through. Serves 10.

Reuben Dip

Jen Burnham, Delaware, OH

16-oz. jar sauerkraut, drained
1/2 lb. deli-style corned beef, shredded
8-oz. pkg. cream cheese, softened
8-oz. pkg. shredded Swiss cheese
1/4 c. Thousand Island salad dressing

Combine all ingredients in a slow cooker. Cover and cook on high setting for 45 minutes, stirring occasionally, just until heated through and cheese is melted. Makes 6 to 7 cups.

Beefy Broccoli Dip

Shelley Turner, Boise, ID

1 lb. ground beef, browned and drained

16-oz. pkg. pasteurized process cheese spread, cubed

10-3/4 oz. can cream of mushroom soup

10-oz. pkg. frozen chopped broccoli, thawed

2 T. salsa

tortilla chips

Combine all ingredients except tortilla chips; mix well. Cover and cook on low setting for 2 to 3 hours, until heated through, stirring after one hour. Serve with tortilla chips. Makes 5-1/2 cups.

Italian Mushrooms

Quick tip

A recipe card holder that you didn't know you had! Place your recipe card in the knife-sharpener side of an electric can opener. It keeps the card clean and at the perfect height for reading.

Ski Club Cheddar Fondue

Ski Club Cheddar Fondue

April Jacobs, Loveland, CO

12-oz. pkg. shredded
  sharp Cheddar cheese
12-oz. pkg. shredded
  Gruyère cheese
3 T. all-purpose flour

1/8 t. nutmeg
1 c. white wine or
  chicken broth
cut-up vegetables, bread
  cubes

Place cheeses in a slow cooker. Sprinkle with flour and nutmeg; toss to coat. Sprinkle wine or broth over cheese mixture. Cover and cook on high setting for 45 minutes to one hour, until cheeses melt. Stir. Turn slow cooker to low setting for serving. Serve with vegetables and bread cubes for dipping. Makes about 15 servings.

Savory Parmesan Crunch Mix

Tonya Shepphard, Galveston, TX

3 c. bite-size crispy corn
  or rice cereal squares
2 c. plain bagel chips,
  broken in half
1-1/2 c. mini pretzel
  twists
1 c. shelled pistachio
  nuts

2 c. oyster crackers
2 T. grated Parmesan
  cheese
1/4 c. butter, melted
1-oz. pkg ranch salad
  dressing mix
1/2 t. garlic powder

In a large slow cooker, combine cereal, chips, pretzels, nuts, crackers and cheese; stir gently and set aside. In a small bowl, stir together remaining ingredients. Drizzle butter mixture over cereal mixture; toss lightly to coat. Cover and cook on low setting for 3 hours. Uncover; stir gently. Cook, uncovered, for an additional 30 minutes. Cool completely; store in an airtight container. Makes about 9 cups.

Real-Deal Reuben Dip

Jessica Kraus, Delaware, OH

16-oz. jar sauerkraut,
  drained
8-oz. pkg. cream cheese,
  softened
2 c. shredded Swiss
  cheese
2 c. deli corned beef,
  shredded

1/4 c. Thousand Island
  salad dressing
1/4 c. diced onion
assorted dippers such
  as crackers and sliced
  party rye

Combine sauerkraut, cheeses, corned beef, onion and dressing in a slow cooker. Cover and cook, stirring occasionally, on high setting for about one to 2 hours, until cheese is melted and dip is smooth. Serve with dippers. Serves 6.

Toffee Fondue

Michelle Riihl, Windom, MN

14-oz. pkg. caramels, unwrapped
1/4 c. milk
1/4 c. strong black coffee
1/2 c. milk chocolate chips

apple wedges, banana chunks, marshmallows, angel food cake cubes

Mix together caramels, milk, coffee and chocolate chips in a small slow cooker. Cover and cook on low setting until melted, about 2 to 3 hours. Stir well. Serve with fruit, marshmallows and cake cubes for dipping. Makes about 10 servings.

Cinnamon-Cocoa Granola

Melody Taynor, Everett, WA

4 c. long-cooking oats, uncooked
2/3 c. honey
1 c. bran cereal
1 c. wheat germ

1/2 c. sesame seed
1/4 c. oil
2 T. baking cocoa
1 t. cinnamon

Combine all ingredients in a slow cooker. Cook on low setting with lid slightly ajar for about 4 hours, stirring occasionally. Cool; store in an airtight container for one to 2 weeks. Makes about 6 cups.

Sugared Walnuts

Connie Fortune, Covington, OH

16-oz. pkg. walnut halves
1/2 c. butter, melted
1/2 c. powdered sugar

1-1/2 t. cinnamon
1/4 t. ground cloves
1/4 t. ground ginger

Preheat slow cooker on high setting for about 15 minutes. Add nuts and butter, stirring to mix well. Add powdered sugar; mix until evenly coated. Cover and cook on high setting for 15 minutes. Reduce heat to low setting. Cook, uncovered, stirring occasionally, for 2 to 3 hours, until nuts are coated with a crisp glaze. Transfer nuts to a serving bowl; set aside. Combine spices in a small bowl and sprinkle over nuts, stirring to coat evenly. Cool before serving. Store in an airtight container. Serves 12 to 16.

Quick tip

Fill a Chinese takeout container with Sugared Walnuts or Cinnamon-Cocoa Granola... always a welcome hostess gift!

Toffee Fondue

Honey Sesame Wings

Honey Sesame Wings

Kimberly Hancock, Murrieta, CA

3 lbs. chicken wings
salt and pepper to taste
2 c. honey
1 c. soy sauce
1/2 c. catsup
1/4 c. oil
2 cloves garlic, minced
Garnish: sesame seed

Place chicken wings on an ungreased broiler pan; sprinkle with salt and pepper. Place pan 4 to 5 inches under broiler. Broil for 10 minutes on each side, or until chicken is golden. Transfer wings to a slow cooker. Combine remaining ingredients except sesame seed; pour over wings. Cover and cook on low setting for 4 to 5 hours, or high setting for 2 to 2-1/2 hours. Arrange on a serving platter; sprinkle with sesame seed. Makes about 2-1/2 dozen.

Fall-Off-the-Bone Hot Wings

Jennie Growden, Cumberland, MD

4 to 5 lbs. chicken wings
seafood seasoning to taste
12-oz. bottle cayenne hot pepper sauce
3 T. butter

Place wings on an aluminum foil-lined baking sheet; sprinkle with seafood seasoning. Bake at 325 degrees for 30 minutes. Sprinkle wings with a little hot sauce; flip wings over and sprinkle with sauce again. Bake for an additional 30 minutes. Combine wings, remaining hot sauce and butter in a slow cooker. Cover and cook on high setting for one hour; reduce heat to low setting and cook for 2 to 3 hours more. Serves 10 to 15.

Spicy Honey-Molasses Wings

Connie Hilty, Pearland, TX

5 lbs. chicken wings
2-1/2 c. spicy catsup
2/3 c. vinegar
1/2 c. plus 2 T. honey
1/2 c. molasses
1 t. salt
1 t. Worcestershire sauce
1/2 t. onion powder
1/2 t. chili powder
Optional: 1/2 to 1 t. smoke-flavored cooking sauce

Arrange chicken wings in a greased 15"x10" jelly-roll pan. Bake, uncovered, at 375 degrees for 30 minutes. Drain; turn wings and bake for an additional 20 to 25 minutes. Remove wings from oven; set aside. Combine remaining ingredients in a large saucepan. Bring to a boil; reduce heat and simmer, uncovered, for 25 to 30 minutes. Arrange one-third of wings in a 5-quart slow cooker; top with one cup sauce. Repeat layers twice. Cover and cook on low setting for 3 to 4 hours; stir before serving. Makes about 4 dozen.

Quick tip

Invite friends & neighbors over for an old-fashioned barbecue. While the kids are tossing a football, and before the grill heats up, load a picnic table with slow-cooker appetizers to nibble on...meatballs, dips, fondue and sausages are just the thing!

Saucy Wieners & Meatballs

Susan Buetow, Du Quoin, IL

1 lb. ground turkey
1/2 c. onion, finely chopped
10 crackers, finely crushed

18-oz. bottle barbecue sauce
12-oz. jar currant or grape jelly
14-oz. pkg. cocktail wieners

In a bowl, mix together turkey, onion and crackers. Form into quarter-size meatballs. Add meatballs to a slow cooker; top with barbecue sauce and jelly. Cover and cook on high setting for 4 hours. Add wieners; stir gently to coat with sauce. Cover and cook for one additional hour. Turn slow cooker to low setting for serving. Serve with toothpicks. Makes about 20 servings.

Hawaiian Meatballs

Teri Lindquist, Gurnee, IL

2 16-oz. pkgs. frozen meatballs
10-oz. jar pineapple preserves

8-oz. bottle barbecue sauce

Place meatballs in a slow cooker. In a bowl, stir together preserves and sauce; pour over meatballs. Gently stir to combine. Cover and cook on low setting for 2 to 3 hours, stirring gently once or twice, until meatballs are hot. Serve with toothpicks. Makes 10 servings.

All-American Hamburger Dip

Cathy Gillilana, Rose Hill, IA

1 lb. ground beef, browned and
  drained
16-oz. pkg. pasteurized process
  cheese spread, cubed

14-1/2 oz. can diced tomatoes with
  green chiles
1/8 t. ground cumin
tortilla chips

Combine all ingredients except chips in a slow cooker. Cover and cook on high setting until cheese is melted, about 30 minutes; stir occasionally. Reduce to low setting to serve. Serve with tortilla chips. Serves 6 to 8.

Hawaiian Meatballs

Buffalo Chicken Potato Skins

Quick side

For a quick and tasty cheese sauce for potato skins, combine one cup evaporated milk and 1/2 cup shredded cheese. Stir over low heat until smooth.

Buffalo Chicken Potato Skins

Melanie Lowe, Dover, DE

1 lb. boneless, skinless
  chicken breasts
1/2 onion, chopped
1 clove garlic, minced
1 stalk celery, chopped
14-1/2 oz. can chicken
  broth
1/3 c. cayenne hot
  pepper sauce

6 baking potatoes, baked
salt and pepper to taste
3/4 c. shredded Cheddar
  cheese
Garnish: blue cheese
  salad dressing

Combine chicken, onion, garlic, celery and broth
in a slow cooker. Cover and cook on high setting for
4 hours, or until chicken is no longer pink in the center.
Remove and shred chicken, reserving 1/2 cup juices
from slow cooker, discarding the rest. Combine
shredded chicken, reserved broth and hot sauce
in slow cooker. Cover and cook on high setting for
30 minutes. Meanwhile, slice potatoes in half
lengthwise; scoop out pulp and save for another recipe.
Place potato skins on a lightly greased baking sheet.
Lightly spray skins with non-stick vegetable spray;
sprinkle with salt and pepper. Bake at 450 degrees
for 10 minutes, or until lightly golden. Evenly divide
chicken mixture and Cheddar cheese among potato
skins. Bake again for about 5 minutes, or until cheese
is melted. Drizzle potatoes with dressing before
serving. Serves 6 to 8.

Barbecued Water Chestnuts

Betty Gretch, Owendale, MI

2 8-oz. cans whole water
  chestnuts, drained
1 lb. bacon, cut in half

1-1/2 c. catsup
6 T. brown sugar, packed
1 T. vinegar

Wrap each chestnut in a piece of bacon; fasten with
a wooden toothpick. Place on an aluminum foil-lined
baking sheet. Bake at 350 degrees for 30 minutes,
or until crisp and golden. Remove chestnuts to a mini
slow cooker; set aside. Combine remaining ingredients
in a saucepan over medium-low heat. Bring to a
simmer; cook for 15 minutes, or until thickened. Spoon
sauce over chestnuts. Turn slow cooker to low setting
for serving. Serves 10.

Nonie's Perfect Party Mix

Donna Reid, Payson, AZ

4 c. doughnut-shaped oat
  cereal
2 c. bite-size crispy rice
  cereal squares
2 c. bite-size crispy
  wheat cereal squares
3 c. pretzel sticks
1-1/2 c. walnuts, broken

13-oz. container salted
  peanuts
1 t. celery salt
1 t. garlic salt
2 T. grated Parmesan
  cheese
1/4 c. butter, melted

Combine cereals, pretzels, nuts, seasonings and cheese
in a slow cooker. Drizzle melted butter over cereal
mixture; stir to coat well. Cover and cook on low
setting for 3 to 3-1/2 hours. Remove lid and cook on
low setting for 30 minutes more. Store in an airtight
container. Makes about 14 cups.

Crabby Artichoke Spread

Kathy Grashoff, Fort Wayne, IN

1 jalapeño pepper, seeded and chopped
1 t. oil
14-oz. can artichokes, drained and chopped

6-oz. can crabmeat, drained
1/2 red pepper, chopped
2 green onions, chopped
1 c. mayonnaise
1/4 c. grated Parmesan cheese

2 t. lemon juice
2 t. Worcestershire sauce
1/2 t. celery seed
assorted crackers

In a skillet over medium heat, sauté jalapeño in oil until tender. Combine in a slow cooker with remaining ingredients except crackers. Cover and cook on low setting for 4 to 6 hours. Serve with crackers. Makes 3 to 4 cups.

Spinach-Artichoke Dip

Rachel Adams, Fort Lewis, WA

14-oz. can artichoke hearts, drained and chopped
2 bunches fresh spinach, chopped
2 8-oz. pkgs. reduced-fat cream cheese, softened and cubed
2-1/2 c. shredded Monterey Jack cheese

2-1/2 c. shredded mozzarella cheese
3 cloves garlic, minced
1/4 t. pepper

pita chips and assorted sliced vegetables for dipping

Combine chopped artichokes, spinach and cheeses in a slow cooker; mix well. Stir in garlic and pepper. Cover and cook on high setting for about one to 2 hours, stirring occasionally, until cheeses are melted and dip is smooth. Reduce heat to low setting to keep warm. Serve with pita chips and sliced vegetables for dipping. Serves 10 to 12.

Spinach-Artichoke Dip

Quick tip

Purchasing a new slow cooker? Look for one that has a "warm" setting...it's perfect for keeping dips toasty throughout potlucks and parties.

Slow-Cooked Scrumptious Salsa

Bacon-Horseradish Dip

Kathy Grashoff, Fort Wayne, IN

3 8-oz. pkgs. cream
  cheese, cubed and
  softened
12-oz. pkg. shredded
  Cheddar cheese
1 c. half-and-half
1/3 c. green onion,
  chopped
3 cloves garlic, minced

3 T. prepared
  horseradish
1 T. Worcestershire
  sauce
1/2 t. pepper
12 slices bacon, crisply
  cooked and crumbled
corn chips or assorted
  crackers

Combine all ingredients except bacon and chips or
crackers in a slow cooker. Cover and cook on low
setting for 4 to 5 hours, or on high setting for 2 to
2-1/2 hours, stirring once halfway through. Stir in
bacon; serve with corn chips or crackers. Makes
7 to 8 cups.

Slow-Cooked Scrumptious Salsa

Marlene Darnell, Newport Beach, CA

10 roma tomatoes, cored
2 cloves garlic
1 onion, cut into wedges
2 jalapeño peppers,
  seeded and chopped

1/4 c. fresh cilantro,
  coarsely chopped
1/2 t. salt

Combine tomatoes, garlic and onion in a slow cooker.
Cover and cook on high setting for 2-1/2 to 3 hours,
until vegetables are tender. Remove crock and let
cool. Combine cooled tomato mixture and remaining
ingredients in a food processor or blender. Process to
desired consistency. May be refrigerated in a covered
container for about one week. Makes about 2 cups.

Rosemary-White Bean Dip

Jo Ann

3/4 c. dried white beans
4 cloves garlic, minced
1 T. fresh rosemary,
  chopped
1 t. red pepper flakes
2 c. vegetable broth
salt to taste
7 T. olive oil

1-1/2 T. lemon juice
1 T. fresh parsley,
  chopped
assorted dippers such
  as crackers, toasted
  baguette slices and
  cherry tomatoes

Combine beans, garlic, rosemary, pepper flakes and
broth in a medium slow cooker. Cover and cook on
high setting for 3 hours, or until beans are soft and
liquid is mostly absorbed. Remove crock and cool.
Place cooled bean mixture into a blender; stir in oil
and lemon juice. Process until dip reaches desired
consistency. Spoon dip into a serving bowl; sprinkle
with parsley. Serve with dippers. Serves 4 to 6.

Bacon-Double Cheese Dip

Lori Roggenbuck, Ubly, MI

8 slices bacon, chopped

2 8-oz. pkgs. cream cheese, softened

1 c. mayonnaise

8-oz. pkg. shredded Swiss cheese

8-oz. pkg. shredded Cheddar cheese

2 green onions, finely chopped

crackers, sliced assorted vegetables

Crisply cook bacon in a skillet over medium heat; drain and set aside. In a bowl, beat cream cheese and mayonnaise until smooth. Stir in Swiss and Cheddar cheeses, green onions and cooked bacon, reserving a little bacon for topping. Spoon dip mixture into a slow cooker. Cover and cook on low setting for 3 hours, or until hot and smooth. Garnish dip with reserved cooked bacon. Serve with crackers and vegetables for dipping. Serves 10 to 12.

Rosemarie's Chili-Cheese Dip

Shirley Padilla, Houston, TX

1-1/2 lbs. ground beef, browned and drained

2 10-oz. cans diced tomatoes with green chiles

1-1/4 oz. pkg. chili seasoning mix

32-oz. pkg. pasteurized process cheese spread, cubed

Mix together ground beef, tomatoes and seasoning in a slow cooker and set aside. Place cheese in a microwave-safe bowl. Microwave on high setting for 5 to 6 minutes until melted, stirring after 3 minutes. Add cheese to ground beef mixture. Cover and cook briefly on low setting until warmed through, stirring occasionally. Keep warm in slow cooker. Makes 9 to 10 cups.

Bacon-Double Cheese Dip

Quick tip

An easy way to crumble ground beef... use a potato masher. It makes browning so quick & easy.

Kara's Sauerkraut Meatballs

Quick tip

Offer a variety of breads when sharing your favorite dip. Rosemary-garlic, tomato-basil, sourdough, focaccia, ciabatta and sesame all have unique flavors...you just might discover a new favorite.

Kara's Sauerkraut Meatballs

Sherry Simon, Watertown, WI

16-oz. can whole-berry cranberry
   sauce
12-oz. jar chili sauce
1-1/2 c. water

1/2 c. brown sugar, packed
16-oz. can sauerkraut, drained
28-oz. pkg. frozen meatballs

In a bowl, mix together sauces, water and brown sugar until combined; set aside. Combine sauerkraut and meatballs in a slow cooker; spoon sauce mixture over all. Stir to mix well. Cover and cook on low setting for 6 hours, or until heated through. Serves 8 to 10.

Finger-Lickin' Ribs

Brad Daugherty, Columbus, OH

3 to 4 lbs. baby back pork ribs
salt and pepper to taste
garlic salt to taste

8-oz. bottle Russian salad dressing
3/4 c. pineapple juice

Slice ribs into several portions to fit into slow cooker; sprinkle with salt and pepper. Arrange in a slow cooker; add enough water just to cover. Cover and cook on high setting for 6 to 7 hours, until tender; drain. Arrange ribs on a broiler pan and sprinkle with garlic salt. Combine salad dressing and pineapple juice in a small bowl; brush ribs with half the sauce. Broil until browned; turn over, brush with remaining sauce and broil other side. Serves 8 to 10.

Speedy Sausages

Denice Louk, Garnett, KS

16-oz. pkg. mini smoked sausages
Optional: 1/2 c. bourbon

1/2 c. grape jelly
2 c. catsup

1/2 c. brown sugar, packed

Combine all ingredients together in a slow cooker. Cook on high setting for one hour.
Makes 10 to 12 servings.

Blue-Ribbon 8-Hour Chili
Kay Little, Diana, TX

3 lbs. lean ground beef
1 T. salt
1 T. pepper
15-oz. can ranch-style beans
14-1/2 oz. can diced tomatoes
10-oz. can diced tomatoes with green chiles
4 8-oz. cans tomato sauce
8 green onions, chopped
1/2 c. onion, minced
4 pickled jalapeños, seeded and minced
1/4 c. pickled jalapeño juice
1/4 c. chili seasoning mix
1 T. ground cumin
2 c. water
Garnish: shredded Cheddar cheese, diced red onion, oyster crackers

Brown beef in a large skillet over medium heat; season with salt and pepper. Drain and spoon beef mixture into a slow cooker. Add undrained beans, undrained tomatoes and remaining ingredients except garnish to slow cooker in order listed; stir. Cover and cook on high setting, stirring occasionally, for 7 to 8 hours. Garnish servings with cheese, onion and crackers. Serves 10 to 12.

Chuck Wagon Stew
Peggy Pelfrey, Fort Riley, KS

1-1/2 lbs. stew beef, cubed
1/2 lb. smoked pork sausage, sliced
1 onion, chopped
3 potatoes, peeled and cubed
28-oz. can barbecue baked beans

Place beef, sausage, onion and potatoes into a slow cooker; mix well. Spoon beans over top. Cover and cook on low setting for 8 to 10 hours, or on high setting 4 to 5 hours. Stir again before serving. Makes 6 servings.

Split Pea Soup
Krista Marshall, Fort Wayne, IN

1 lb. cooked ham, diced
1 lb. carrots, peeled and finely diced
1 onion, finely diced
2 12-oz. pkgs. dried split peas
salt and pepper to taste

Combine ham, carrots, onion and dried peas in a slow cooker. Add enough water to cover. Cover and cook on high setting for 6 to 8 hours, stirring occasionally, until peas are tender and soup becomes very thick. Add additional water to reach desired consistency, if desired; season with salt and pepper. Serves 8 to 10.

Chuck Wagon Stew

Chicken Taco Soup

Chicken Taco Soup

Janet Allen, Hauser, ID

1 onion, chopped
16-oz. can chili beans
15-oz. can black beans
15-oz. can corn
2 10-oz. cans diced tomatoes with green chiles
8-oz. can tomato sauce
12-oz. can beer or non-alcoholic beer
1-1/4 oz. pkg. taco seasoning mix
3 boneless, skinless chicken breasts
Garnish: shredded Cheddar cheese, crushed tortilla chips
Optional: sour cream

In a slow cooker, mix together onion, beans, corn, diced tomatoes with juice, tomato sauce and beer. Add seasoning mix; stir to blend. Lightly press chicken breasts into mixture in slow cooker until partially covered. Cover and cook on low setting for 5 hours. Remove chicken from slow cooker; shred and return to soup. Cover and cook for an additional 2 hours. Top servings of soup with cheese, crushed chips and sour cream, if desired. Serves 8.

French Onion Soup

Kristen Taylor, Fort Smith, AR

1/4 c. butter, sliced
1/4 c. olive oil
4 sweet onions, thinly sliced
1/4 c. all-purpose flour
salt and pepper to taste
3 32-oz. containers beef broth
1 c. red wine or beef broth
8 to 10 slices baguette or French bread
8 to 10 slices baby Swiss cheese

Melt butter with olive oil in a large skillet over medium heat. Add onions; cover and cook until onions are soft and translucent. Sprinkle with flour; cook and stir until onions are golden. Season with salt and pepper. Spoon onions into a large slow cooker. Add broth and wine or broth. Cover and cook on low setting for 7 to 8 hours. Shortly before serving time, arrange bread slices on a baking sheet. Top with cheese slices; broil until bread is toasted and cheese is melted. Ladle soup into bowls; top each with a toasted bread slice. Makes 8 to 10 servings.

Simple Vegetable Soup

Connie Hilty, Pearland, TX

4 c. water
2 c. tomato juice
2 c. frozen green beans
1 c. cabbage, sliced
2 carrots, peeled and sliced
1 onion, sliced
1 stalk celery, sliced
2 cubes beef or vegetable bouillon
1 t. salt
pepper to taste
Optional: 1 T. soy sauce, 1 t. sugar or sugar substitute

Combine all ingredients in a slow cooker. Cover and cook on low setting for 4 to 8 hours, until vegetables are tender. Serves 6.

Quick tip

When freezing soup, leave a little headspace at the top…it needs room to expand as it freezes.

Vegetarian Cincinnati Chili

Leatha Sarvo, Cincinnati, OH

46-oz. can tomato juice
16-oz. can kidney beans, drained and rinsed
1 onion, chopped
2 T. chili powder
1-1/2 t. white vinegar
1 t. allspice

1 t. cinnamon
1 t. pepper
1 t. ground cumin
1/8 t. garlic powder
1/4 t. Worcestershire sauce
5 bay leaves

Combine all ingredients in a slow cooker. Cover and cook on low setting for 5 hours. Discard bay leaves before serving. Serves 6.

Meatless Mexican Chili

Laura Witham, Anchorage, AK

2 15-oz. cans ranch-style beans
2 10-oz. cans diced tomatoes with green chiles
15-1/2 oz. can white hominy, drained
15-1/2 oz. can golden hominy, drained

1-oz. pkg. ranch salad dressing mix
3 c. vegetable broth
Garnish: shredded Cheddar cheese, crushed tortilla chips

Combined all ingredients except broth and garnish in a slow cooker. Stir in broth; cover and cook on high setting for 6 hours, or on low setting for 8 hours. Serve individual portions sprinkled with cheese and chips. Serves 6 to 8.

Very Veggie Chili

Bobbie Sofia, Lake Havasu City, AZ

1 T. olive oil
2 c. carrots, peeled and diced
1 c. celery, diced
1 onion, diced
16-oz. pkg. sliced mushrooms
2 zucchini, chopped
2 yellow squash, chopped
1 T. chili powder
1 t. dried basil

1 t. pepper
4 8-oz. cans tomato sauce
1 c. vegetable broth
2 14-1/2 oz. cans diced tomatoes
2 15-oz. cans black beans, drained and rinsed
2 15-oz. cans dark red kidney beans, drained and rinsed
Optional: 1 c. frozen corn, 2 c. kale or spinach

Heat oil in a large skillet over medium heat. Sauté carrots, celery and onion in oil for 5 minutes. Stir in mushrooms, zucchini and squash; sauté for 3 minutes. Sprinkle with seasonings; cook for 5 minutes. Add tomato sauce and broth to a slow cooker. Add tomatoes with juice, beans, carrot mixture and corn, if using. Cover and cook on low setting for 8 hours. Add kale or spinach during the last hour of cooking, if using. Serves 6 to 8.

Very Veggie Chili

🥄🍴🔪 Quick side

Fluffy dumplings are tasty in any hearty soup. About 30 minutes before soup is done, mix up 2 cups biscuit baking mix with 3/4 cup milk. Drop by tablespoonfuls onto simmering soup. Cover and cook on high setting for 20 to 25 minutes...done!

Stuffed Green Pepper Soup

Stuffed Green Pepper Soup

Darlene Jones, Milford, MA

1 lb. extra-lean ground
  beef
1 c. onion, diced
14-1/2 oz. can diced
  tomatoes
2 c. green peppers,
  chopped

15-oz. can tomato sauce
3 c. water
1 T. beef bouillon
  granules
1/2 t. dried basil
1/2 t. dried oregano
1 c. cooked brown rice

In a skillet over medium heat, brown beef with onion.
Drain; transfer to a slow cooker. Add undrained
tomatoes and remaining ingredients. Cover and
cook on low setting for 6 to 8 hours. Makes 8 servings.

Sweet Potato Chili

Shelley Turner, Boise, ID

2 sweet potatoes, peeled
  and cut into 2-inch
  chunks
1 yellow onion, diced
1 red pepper, chopped
2 cloves garlic, minced
14-1/2 oz. can diced
  fire-roasted tomatoes

15-oz. can kidney beans,
  drained and rinsed
1 T. chili powder
1 t. paprika
1/2 t. salt
1-1/2 c. water
Garnish: shredded
  Cheddar cheese

Combine sweet potato, onion, red pepper and garlic in a
slow cooker. Stir in undrained tomatoes and remaining
ingredients except garnish. Cover and cook on low
setting for 6 to 8 hours, until sweet potato is tender.
Using a spoon, mash a few sweet potato cubes against
side of crock to thicken soup. Top servings with cheese.
Serves 6 to 8.

Savory Beef Stew

Jennifer Wilson, Saginaw, TX

1 t. oil
1 lb. boneless beef round
  steak, cubed
3 potatoes, peeled and
  cubed
1 c. baby carrots
14-1/2 oz. can beef broth

14-1/2 oz. can stewed
  tomatoes
.75-oz. pkg. garlic & herb
  salad dressing mix
2/3 to 1 c. water
hot buttered noodles

Heat oil in a skillet over medium heat. Add steak;
brown on both sides. Place steak, drippings and
remaining ingredients in a slow cooker. Add water
to desired consistency. Cover and cook on low setting
for 8 to 10 hours. Serve over hot buttered noodles.
Serves 4 to 6.

Hearty Pumpkin Chili

Claire Bertram, Lexington, KY

1 T. oil
1 lb. ground turkey
1 c. onion, chopped
1 c. green and/or yellow pepper, diced

1 clove garlic, minced
14-1/2 oz. can diced tomatoes
15-oz. can pumpkin
1-1/2 T. chili powder
1/2 t. pepper

1/8 t. salt
Garnish: shredded Cheddar cheese, sour cream

Heat oil in a skillet over medium heat. Add turkey, onion, green and/or yellow pepper and garlic; cook until turkey is browned and vegetables are tender. Spoon turkey mixture into a slow cooker. Stir in undrained tomatoes, pumpkin and seasonings. Cover and cook on low setting for 4 to 5 hours. Garnish individual servings with cheese and sour cream. Makes 4 to 6 servings.

Lentil Chili

Ashley Gaudiano, Stamford, CT

16-oz. pkg. dried brown lentils
7 c. low-sodium vegetable broth
1 yellow onion, chopped
1 red pepper, chopped

4 to 5 cloves garlic, minced
2 T. chili powder
2 15-oz. cans diced tomatoes, drained

1/4 c. fresh cilantro, chopped
Garnish: sour cream, shredded Cheddar cheese

Soak lentils in water for 2 hours up to overnight; drain. Combine lentils and remaining ingredients except cilantro and garnish in a slow cooker. Cover and cook on low setting for 4 to 6 hours, until lentils are tender; stir in cilantro just before serving. Top bowls with a dollop of sour cream and a sprinkle of cheese. Serves 8 to 10.

Quick tip

Root vegetables like sweet potatoes, carrots and onions grow tender and sweet with all-day slow cooking. Give parsnips a try too...delicious!

Hearty Pumpkin Chili

Old-Fashioned Bean Soup

Beef Barley Soup

Lynne McKaige, Savage, MN

2 c. carrots, peeled and thinly sliced
1 c. celery, thinly sliced
3/4 c. green pepper, diced
1 c. onion, diced

1 lb. stew beef cubes
1/2 c. pearl barley, uncooked
1/4 c. fresh parsley, chopped
3 cubes beef bouillon
2 T. catsup

1 t. salt
3/4 t. dried basil
5 c. water

Layer vegetables, beef and barley in a slow cooker; add seasonings. Pour water over all; do not stir. Cover and cook on low setting for 9 to 11 hours. Makes 4 to 6 servings.

Old-Fashioned Bean Soup

Kathleen Poritz, Burlington, WI

16-oz. pkg. dried navy beans
2 qts. water
1 meaty ham bone
1 onion, chopped

1/2 c. celery leaves, chopped
5 whole peppercorns
salt to taste
Optional: bay leaf

Cover beans with water in a large soup pot; soak overnight. Drain. Combine beans, 2 quarts water and remaining ingredients in a slow cooker. Cover and cook on low setting for 10 to 12 hours, or on high setting for 5 to 6 hours. Remove ham bone; dice meat and return to slow cooker. Discard bay leaf, if using. Makes 8 to 10 servings.

Wisconsin Bacon-Potato Soup

Debbie Hundley, Barron, WI

5 lbs. potatoes, peeled and chopped
1/2 lb. bacon, crisply cooked and crumbled

1 onion, chopped
8-oz. container sour cream
3 14-1/2 oz. cans chicken broth
10-3/4 oz. cream of chicken soup

Combine all ingredients in a slow cooker. Cover and cook on low setting for 8 to 10 hours, or on high setting for 4 to 5 hours. Serves 6 to 8.

Corny Bacon Chowder

Elizabeth Cisneros, Chino Hills, CA

2 T. butter	1 c. milk
6 slices bacon, chopped	28-oz. can creamed corn
1/2 red onion, minced	14-oz. can corn
2 T. all-purpose flour	1/2 red pepper, chopped
1/4 t. salt	1/2 green pepper, chopped
1/4 t. pepper	
1/8 t. cayenne pepper	1/2 t. dried parsley

Melt butter in a skillet over medium heat. Add bacon and onion; sauté until bacon is crisp. Add flour, salt, pepper and cayenne pepper to skillet; mix thoroughly. Add milk; cook and stir until thickened. Transfer to a slow cooker; add remaining ingredients. Cover and cook on low setting for 2 to 4 hours. Serves 4 to 6.

Southern BBQ Bean Soup

Tori Willis, Champaign, IL

16-oz. pkg. dried Great Northern beans	2 lbs. beef short ribs, cut into serving-size pieces
3/4 c. onion, chopped	1 c. barbecue sauce
1/8 t. pepper	1 to 2 t. salt

Cover beans with water in a large soup pot; soak overnight. Drain. Combine beans, onion, pepper and short ribs in a slow cooker; add enough water to cover. Cover and cook on low setting for 10 to 12 hours. Remove short ribs; cut meat from bones. Return meat to slow cooker; stir in sauce and salt to taste. Cover and cook on high setting for an additional 20 minutes, or until warmed through. Serves 6 to 8.

Italian Meatball Soup

Alice Hardin, Antioch, CA

16-oz. pkg. frozen Italian-style meatballs	1 c. potato, peeled and chopped
2 14-oz. cans beef broth	1/2 c. onion, chopped
2 14-1/2 oz. cans diced tomatoes with Italian herbs	1/4 t. garlic pepper
	16-oz. pkg. frozen mixed vegetables

In a slow cooker, mix frozen meatballs with all ingredients except frozen mixed vegetables. Cover and cook on low setting for 9 to 11 hours. Stir in frozen mixed vegetables. Increase setting to high; cover and cook for one additional hour, or until vegetables are tender. Makes 4 to 6 servings.

Southern BBQ Bean Soup

Pantry Tomato Soup

Quick tip

Refrigerate slow-cooked foods or leftovers within 2 hours of turning off the slow cooker.

Pantry Tomato Soup

Christina Sheppard, Centerville, OH

14-1/2 oz. can diced tomatoes with basil, garlic and oregano
28-oz. can tomato sauce
14-1/2 oz. can tomato soup
14-1/2 oz. can chicken broth
Garnish: sour cream, grated Parmesan cheese, fish-shaped crackers

Combine undrained tomatoes, sauce, soup and broth in a slow cooker. Cover and cook on low setting for 2 hours, or until heated through. Garnish as desired. Makes 6 to 8 servings.

Loaded Potato Soup

Sherry Webb, Ridgeway, VA

5 lbs. potatoes, peeled, diced and cooked
2 14-1/2 oz. cans chicken broth
12-oz. can evaporated milk
8-oz. container sour cream
1/2 c. butter, sliced
2 T. salt-free herb seasoning
16-oz. pkg. shredded Cheddar cheese
16-oz. pkg. shredded Pepper Jack cheese
4 to 6 green onions, chopped
3-oz. pkg. bacon bits
saltine crackers

Place potatoes in a 7-quart slow cooker. Add broth, evaporated milk, sour cream, butter, seasoning and cheeses; stir well. Cover and cook on low setting for 4 hours, stirring occasionally. Add onions. Cover and continue cooking for one hour. Serve topped with bacon bits and crackers. Serves 15 to 20.

Pig-in-a-Poke Ham Soup

Sonia Hawkins, Amarillo, TX

4 14-1/2 oz. cans green beans
1 meaty ham bone
4 potatoes, peeled and quartered
1 onion, sliced
pepper to taste

In a slow cooker, combine undrained green beans and remaining ingredients. Cover and cook on high setting for one hour. Reduce to low setting; cover and cook for 6 to 7 hours, until the meat falls off the bone. Remove ham bone; dice meat and return to slow cooker. Makes 10 servings.

Slow-Cooker Turkey Chili

Barbie Hall, Salisbury, MD

2 lbs. ground turkey
2 onions, chopped
3 cloves garlic, minced
28-oz. can diced tomatoes
28-oz. can tomato purée
15-1/2 oz. can kidney beans, drained and rinsed
15-1/2 oz. can chili beans
2-1/2 T. chili powder
1 T. ground cumin
1/2 t. cayenne pepper
1 t. salt

In a skillet over medium heat, brown turkey; drain. Transfer to a slow cooker, reserving 2 tablespoons drippings in the skillet. In the same skillet, cook onions until translucent. Add garlic; cook for one minute longer. Add onion mixture and remaining ingredients to slow cooker; stir to combine. Cover and cook on low setting for 6 to 8 hours. Serves 8.

Quick tip

There's no such thing as too much chili! Top hot dogs and baked potatoes with extra chili...spoon into flour tortillas and sprinkle with shredded cheese for quick burritos.

Italian Chicken Stew

Lisanne Miller, Canton, MS

3 to 4 boneless, skinless chicken breasts
2 28-oz. cans stewed tomatoes
20-oz. pkg. frozen Italian vegetables
1 clove garlic, minced
16-oz. pkg. rigatoni pasta, uncooked
Garnish: shredded mozzarella cheese, grated Parmesan cheese

Place chicken, tomatoes, vegetables and garlic in a slow cooker. Cover and cook on low setting for 4 to 5 hours. About 35 minutes before cooking is complete, top stew with uncooked pasta; do not stir. Cover and finish cooking about 35 minutes. Pasta will thicken the stew as it cooks. Garnish portions with cheeses. Makes 4 to 5 servings.

1-2-3 Chunky Turkey Soup

Melody Chencharick, Julian, PA

3 c. turkey or chicken broth
3/4 to 1 c. cooked turkey, cubed
1/2 c. frozen baby lima beans
1 potato, peeled and cubed
2 stalks celery, chopped
1/2 c. onion, chopped
1/3 c. carrot, peeled and sliced
1/2 c. spiral pasta, uncooked
1 T. fresh parsley, snipped
1 t. pepper

Combine all ingredients in a slow cooker; stir well. Cover and cook on low setting for 6 to 8 hours. Serves 4.

Italian Chicken Stew

Green Chile Stew

Green Chile Stew

Linda Neel, Lovington, NM

1 to 1-1/2 lbs. boneless
  pork, cubed
2 16-oz. cans pinto beans
2 14-1/2 oz. cans
  Mexican-style diced
  tomatoes

2 4-oz. cans diced green
  chiles
15-1/2 oz. can hominy,
  drained
1 t. ground cumin
salt and pepper to taste

Place pork in a slow cooker. Top with remaining
ingredients; stir. Cover and cook on high setting
for 4 to 5 hours. Serves 4.

Mexican Minestrone

Ashley Billings, Shamong, NJ

3 14-oz. cans vegetable
  broth
2 15-1/2 oz. cans
  reduced-sodium black
  beans, drained and
  rinsed
15-oz. can garbanzo
  beans, drained and
  rinsed

2 to 3 tomatoes, chopped
2 c. potatoes, peeled and
  diced
2 c. frozen green beans
1 c. frozen corn
1 c. salsa
Garnish: sour cream

In a slow cooker, combine all ingredients except
garnish; stir gently to mix. Cover and cook on low
setting for 9 to 11 hours, or on high setting for 4-1/2 to
5-1/2 hours. Garnish individual bowls with sour cream.
Makes 6 to 8 servings.

Rio Grande Green Pork Chili

Debby Heatwole, Canadian, TX

3 lbs. boneless pork
  steak, cubed
1 clove garlic, minced
3 T. olive oil
1/2 c. all-purpose flour
2 14-1/2 oz. cans beef
  broth
32-oz. can tomato juice
14-1/2 oz. can crushed
  tomatoes

7-oz. can diced green
  chiles
4-oz. can chopped
  jalapeño peppers
1/3 c. dried parsley
1/4 c. lemon juice
2 t. ground cumin
1 t. sugar
1/4 t. ground cloves

In a heavy skillet over medium heat, sauté pork
and garlic in oil. Add flour, stirring until thoroughly
mixed. Drain; place browned pork in a slow cooker.
Add remaining ingredients; cover and cook on low
setting for 6 to 8 hours, until pork is tender. Serves
12 to 14.

Divine Seafood Chowder

Audrey Laudenat, East Haddam, CT

1 onion, sliced
4 potatoes, peeled and sliced
minced garlic to taste
1 t. dill weed
2 T. butter, diced
1 c. clam juice, heated to boiling
15-oz. can creamed corn
salt and pepper to taste
1/2 lb. haddock or cod fillets
1/2 lb. medium shrimp, peeled, cleaned and halved
1 c. light cream, warmed

Layer all ingredients except cream in a slow cooker, placing fish and shrimp on top. Cover and cook on high setting for one hour; reduce setting to low and cook for 3 hours. Gently stir in cream just before serving. Makes 4 to 6 servings.

Hearty Fish Chowder

Marlene Campbell, Millinocket, ME

1 onion, chopped
1 carrot, peeled and sliced
2 stalks celery, sliced
1/4 c. water
2 lbs. haddock
10-3/4 oz. can cream of shrimp soup
1-1/4 c. milk
1/4 t. dried thyme
1/4 t. pepper

Combine onion, carrot and celery in a slow cooker. Add water; cover and cook on high setting for 2 hours. Cut fish into large pieces, about 3 inches square. Place fish pieces on top of vegetables. Combine remaining ingredients in a bowl; pour over fish. Reduce heat to low. Cover and cook for 3-3/4 hours, or until fish flakes easily. Uncover; break fish into smaller pieces with a fork and stir. Cover; turn off slow cooker and let stand for 15 minutes before serving. Serves 4.

Cream of Crab Soup

Bernice Hamburg, Baltimore, MD

4 10-3/4 oz. cans cream of celery soup
1 lb. refrigerated lump or special crabmeat
1 qt. half-and-half
2 T. butter, sliced
2 T. seafood seasoning
Optional: milk

Combine all ingredients except milk in a large slow cooker; stir. Cover and cook on high setting for 4 to 6 hours, stirring frequently to prevent sticking. Soup will start out thin, but will thicken as it sets; stir in some milk if too thick. Serves 8 to 12.

Quick tip

Arrange seashells and beach glass from your last vacation on a cake stand. Tuck in some tea lights too...a sweet reminder of happy family times!

Hearty Fish Chowder

Spicy Spinach-Sausage Soup

Spicy Spinach-Sausage Soup

Patricia Skalka, Medford, NJ

1-1/2 lbs. ground hot
   Italian sausage
48-oz. can stewed
   tomatoes
49-oz. can chicken broth
1 onion, chopped
8-oz. pkg. sliced
   mushrooms

16-oz. pkg. baby carrots,
   sliced
10-oz. pkg. frozen
   chopped spinach,
   thawed
1 t. garlic pepper
1/4 c. grated Parmesan
   cheese

Brown sausage in a skillet over medium heat; drain.
Combine cooked sausage, undrained tomatoes and
remaining ingredients in a slow cooker; mix well.
Cover and cook on low setting for 8 to 9 hours.
Serves 8.

Easy Cheesy Potato Soup

Tami Harrison, Bradford, OH

32-oz. pkg. frozen
   Southern-style diced
   potatoes
1/2 c. onion, chopped
32-oz. container chicken
   broth
1 c. water
3 T. all-purpose flour

salt and pepper to taste
1 c. milk
8-oz. pkg. shredded
   Cheddar cheese
1/4 lb. bacon, crisply
   cooked and crumbled
Garnish: sliced green
   onions

Combine potatoes, onion, broth and water in a slow
cooker. Cover and cook on low setting for 6 to 7 hours.
In a bowl, combine flour, salt, pepper and milk; mix
well. Pour flour mixture into slow cooker; increase to
high setting. Cover and cook for 20 to 30 minutes, until
soup has thickened. Add cheese, stirring until melted.
Garnish servings with crumbled bacon and green
onions. Serves 6 to 8.

Chicken & Broccoli Chowder

Susie Backus, Delaware, OH

1 lb. boneless, skinless
   chicken thighs, cubed
14-1/2 oz. can chicken
   broth
1/2 c. water
1 c. baby carrots, sliced
1 c. sliced mushrooms
1/2 c. onion, chopped

1/4 t. garlic powder
1/8 t. dried thyme
10-3/4 oz. can cream of
   chicken & broccoli soup
1/2 c. milk
3 T. all-purpose flour
10-oz. pkg. frozen
   broccoli, thawed

Combine chicken, broth, water, carrots, mushrooms,
onion and seasonings in a slow cooker; mix well.
Cover and cook on low setting for 7 to 9 hours. In a
small bowl, whisk together soup, milk and flour; stir
into slow cooker along with broccoli. Cover and cook
an additional 30 minutes, or until broccoli is tender.
Makes 4 to 6 servings.

Quick tip

When serving soups and stews, stack two
or three cake stands, then fill each tier with a
different type of roll for guests to try...they'll
love the variety.

Vegetarian Vegetable Soup

Barb Bargdill, Gooseberry Patch

32-oz. bottle cocktail vegetable
  juice
2 16-oz. pkgs. frozen mixed soup
  vegetables
14-oz. can vegetable broth

3 c. water
6-oz. can tomato paste
1/2 c. onion, chopped
1 T. garlic, chopped

1/2 t. Italian seasoning
1 t. salt
1 t. sugar

Combine all ingredients in a large slow cooker; stir well. Cover and cook on low setting for 6 to 8 hours. Makes 12 to 15 servings.

Chicken & Quinoa Chili

Lori Rosenberg, University Heights, OH

2 boneless, skinless chicken
  breasts
28-oz. can diced tomatoes
14-1/2 oz. can diced tomatoes with
  green chiles
15-1/2 oz. can chili beans, drained
  and rinsed

15-1/2 oz. can black beans,
  drained and rinsed
15-1/4 oz. can corn, drained
2 c. chicken broth
1 c. quinoa, uncooked and rinsed
2 to 3 t. chili powder

2 t. garlic powder
2 t. ground cumin
1/2 t. red pepper flakes
Garnish: chopped avocado, salsa,
  other toppings

Place chicken in a large slow cooker. Add undrained tomatoes and remaining ingredients except garnish; stir gently. Cover and cook on low setting for 6 to 8 hours, or on high setting for 4 to 6 hours. Remove chicken and shred with 2 forks; return to slow cooker. Serve chili garnished as desired. Makes 8 servings.

Vegetarian Vegetable Soup

Black Bean Chili

Black Bean Chili

Darrell Lawry, Kissimmee, FL

1-lb. pork tenderloin
3 15-1/2 oz. cans black beans, drained and rinsed
16-oz. jar chunky salsa
1/2 c. chicken broth
1 green pepper, chopped

1 onion, chopped
2 t. chili powder
1 t. ground cumin
1 t. dried oregano
Garnish: sour cream, diced tomatoes

Place pork in a lightly greased slow cooker; add remaining ingredients except garnish. Cover and cook on low setting for 8 hours, or on high setting for 4 hours. Shred pork; return to slow cooker. Garnish servings with dollops of sour cream and diced tomatoes. Serves 4 to 6.

Cheesy White Chicken Chili

Holly Child, Parker, CO

4 to 6 boneless, skinless chicken breasts, cooked and cubed
6 c. chicken broth
4 16-oz. cans Great Northern beans, drained and rinsed

4-oz. can green chiles
1 onion, chopped
1 T. garlic, minced
1 T. ground cumin
1-1/2 t. dried oregano
1-1/2 c. shredded Monterey Jack cheese

Combine all ingredients except cheese in a large slow cooker. Cover and cook on high setting for 4 to 6 hours. During the last hour, turn slow cooker to low setting. Stir in cheese; let stand for several minutes, until cheese is completely melted. Makes 8 servings.

Pinto-Pork Chili

Michelle Farmer, Evansville, IN

1 lb. ground pork
28-oz. can diced tomatoes
15-1/2 oz. can black beans
16-oz. can pinto beans
15-1/2 oz. white beans

1-1/4 oz. pkg. chili seasoning mix
1 onion, chopped
1 green pepper, chopped
Garnish: shredded Cheddar cheese, saltine crackers

Brown pork in a skillet over medium heat; drain. Combine pork, undrained tomatoes, undrained beans and remaining ingredients except garnish in a slow cooker. Cover and cook on low setting for 6 to 8 hours. Garnish servings with cheese and crackers, if desired. Serves 6 to 8.

Quick tip

Simple slow-cooker recipes are ideal for older children just learning to cook. With supervision, they can learn to use paring knives, can openers and hot mitts…and they'll be oh-so-proud to serve the dinner they've prepared!

Sausage & Tortellini Soup

Diana Krol, Nickerson, KS

1 lb. Italian pork sausage links, cut into bite-size pieces
1 onion, chopped
1 green pepper, chopped
2 cloves garlic, minced
14-1/2 oz. can green beans
1 T. dried parsley
2 t. dried oregano
14-1/2 oz. can chicken broth
2 32-oz. cans tomato juice
9-oz. pkg. frozen cheese tortellini, uncooked

Sauté sausage, onion, green pepper and garlic in a skillet over medium heat until browned; drain. Combine sausage mixture, beans with liquid and remaining ingredients except tortellini in a slow cooker. Cover and cook on low setting for 4 hours; stir in tortellini. Cover and cook for 30 more minutes, or until heated through. Serves 8 to 10.

Zuppa Pizzeria

Melinda Schadler, Fargo, ND

1 lb. ground Italian pork sausage, browned
14-1/2 oz. can diced tomatoes with garlic, basil & oregano
4-oz. can sliced mushrooms
14-1/2 oz. can beef broth
2-1/2 oz. pkg. pepperoni slices, diced
1 green pepper, diced
1 onion, diced
1 c. water
1 T. Italian seasoning
Garnish: 1 c. shredded mozzarella cheese

Brown sausage in a skillet over medium heat; drain. Combine sausage, undrained tomatoes, undrained mushrooms and remaining ingredients except garnish in a slow cooker; stir to mix well. Cover and cook on low setting for 4 to 6 hours, until vegetables are tender. Ladle soup into bowls; sprinkle with cheese. Serves 6 to 8.

Sausage & Tortellini Soup

Quick side

Turn hot dog buns into garlic bread sticks in a jiffy! Spread with softened butter, sprinkle with garlic salt and broil until toasty. Thrifty and tasty!

White Chili

Wendy West Hickey, Pittsburgh, PA

16-oz. pkg. dried Great Northern beans
2 lbs. boneless, skinless chicken breasts, cubed
14-1/2 oz. can chicken broth

1 c. water
1 onion, chopped
3 cloves garlic, minced
2 4-oz. cans chopped green chiles
2 t. ground cumin

1-1/2 t. cayenne pepper
1 t. dried oregano
1/2 t. salt
Garnish: shredded Monterey Jack cheese, chopped green onions

Cover beans with water in a large soup pot and soak overnight; drain. In a slow cooker, combine beans with remaining ingredients except garnish and stir. Cover and cook on low setting for 10 to 12 hours, or on high setting for 5 to 6 hours, stirring occasionally. Garnish individual portions as desired. Serves 6 to 8.

White Chili

Slow-Cooker Steak Chili

Mignonne Gardner, Pleasant Grove, UT

2 T. oil
2 lbs. beef round steak, cut into
   1-inch cubes
1-1/2 c. onion, chopped
2 cloves garlic, minced
1-1/3 c. water, divided
1 c. celery, chopped

2 15-oz. cans kidney beans,
   drained and rinsed
2 14-1/2 oz. cans diced tomatoes
16-oz. jar salsa
15-oz. can tomato sauce
1-1/2 T. chili powder
1 t. ground cumin

1 t. dried oregano
1/2 t. pepper
2 T. all-purpose flour
2 T. cornmeal
Garnish: diced tomatoes, sour
   cream, crushed tortilla chips,
   shredded Cheddar cheese

Heat oil in a large sauté pan over medium heat; add steak, onion and garlic. Cook over medium heat until steak is browned and onion and garlic are translucent. With a slotted spoon, remove steak, onion and garlic to a slow cooker, leaving juices behind in pan. Add one cup water, celery, beans, tomatoes with juice, salsa, tomato sauce and seasonings to slow cooker; stir. Cover and cook on low setting for 8 hours. Shortly before serving time, whisk together flour, cornmeal and remaining 1/3 cup water until smooth. Add mixture to simmering chili; stir for 2 minutes, until thickened. Garnish as desired. Serves 8.

Barbecue Beef Chili

Sherry Gordon, Arlington Heights, IL

7 t. chili powder
1 T. garlic powder
2 t. celery seed
1 t. pepper
1/2 t. cayenne pepper
4-lb. beef brisket

1 green pepper, chopped
1 onion, chopped
12-oz. bottle chili sauce
1/2 c. barbecue sauce
1/4 c. Worcestershire sauce
1 c. catsup

1/3 c. brown sugar, packed
1/4 c. cider vinegar
1 t. dry mustard
15-1/2 oz. can hot chili beans
15-1/2 oz. can Great Northern
   beans, drained and rinsed

In a bowl, combine seasonings. Rub seasoning mixture on all sides of brisket; place in a slow cooker. In a separate bowl, combine remaining ingredients except beans; mix well and spoon over brisket. Cover and cook on high setting for 5 to 6 hours, until brisket is very tender. Remove brisket from slow cooker; shred with 2 forks. Return shredded brisket to slow cooker; reduce to low setting. Stir in beans; cover and cook for one hour, or until heated through. Serves 10 to 12.

Mushroom-Chicken Stew

Jamie Johnson, Columbus, OH

2 T. oil

6 boneless, skinless chicken thighs, cut into 1-1/2 inch strips

salt and pepper to taste

1 leek, chopped

4 c. chicken broth

8-oz. pkg. sliced mushrooms

1-1/2 c. baby carrots, halved

3/4 c. frozen peas

Heat oil in a skillet over medium heat. Season chicken with salt and pepper. Cook chicken in oil until golden on both sides, about 5 minutes per side. Remove chicken to a slow cooker; set aside. Add leek to drippings in pan; sauté until tender. Stir in broth and scrape up any browned bits from skillet. Transfer leek mixture to slow cooker; stir in mushrooms and carrots. Cover and cook on low setting for 6 to 8 hours. Break up chicken into bite-size pieces with a spoon; stir in peas. Cook for 5 minutes, or until heated through. Serves 4 to 6.

Rustic Beef Stew

Jill Valentine, Jackson, TN

3 lbs. stew beef cubes

salt and pepper to taste

1 T. oil

2 14-1/2 oz. cans beef broth

10-1/2 oz. can beef consommé

2 c. Burgundy wine or beef broth

1 c. water

1 t. dry mustard

1 t. dried thyme

1/2 lb. baby carrots

5 redskin potatoes, cut into chunks

1/2 lb. pearl onions, peeled

Optional: 2 T. cornstarch and 1 T. water

Sprinkle beef with salt and pepper. Heat oil in a skillet over medium heat. Brown beef in oil; drain and set aside. Combine broth, consommé, wine or broth, water, mustard and thyme in a slow cooker; stir. Add beef, carrots, potatoes and onions to broth mixture; mix well. Cover and cook on low setting for 6 hours, or until vegetables and beef are tender. If a thicker stew is desired, mix together cornstarch and water in a small bowl; stir into stew. Cook, stirring occasionally, until thickened, about 20 minutes. Serves 12.

Quick tip

Need to add a little zing to a soup or stew? Just add a splash of Worcestershire sauce, lemon juice or flavored vinegar.

Mushroom-Chicken Stew

Quick tip

Tote along a vintage thermos filled with hot soup on a cool-weather nature walk...it'll really hit the spot! Before ladling in the soup, prewarm the thermos with hot water for 10 minutes.

Down-Home Chicken Noodle Soup

Down-Home Chicken Noodle Soup

Sarah Roy, Tyndall AFB, FL

4 14-1/2 oz. cans chicken broth
16-oz. pkg. baby carrots
4 stalks celery, cut into 1/2-inch pieces
1 T. fresh parsley, minced

1/2 t. pepper
1/2 t. cayenne pepper
2-1/2 lbs. boneless, skinless chicken breasts
3/4 c. onion, finely chopped

1-1/2 t. mustard seed
2 cloves garlic, halved
8-oz. pkg. egg noodles, cooked

Combine broth, carrots, celery, parsley and peppers in a slow cooker. Place chicken in broth mixture; set aside. Combine onion, mustard seed and garlic in a thick square of cheesecloth; tie into a bundle. Add spice bundle to slow cooker. Cover and cook on low setting for 5 to 6 hours. Remove chicken from slow cooker; shred and return to slow cooker. Discard spice bundle. Stir cooked noodles into soup; cover and cook for 15 minutes, or until warmed through. Serves 6 to 8.

Italian Sub Cream Soup

Stephanie Carlson, Sioux Falls, SD

1 T. olive oil
1 lb. ground Italian pork sausage
3-1/2 oz. pkg. sliced pepperoni, slices quartered
1/4 lb. deli sliced salami, slices quartered
1 green pepper, diced
1 onion, diced

2 cloves garlic, minced
2 to 3 T. all-purpose flour
28-oz. can diced tomatoes
4 c. chicken broth
salt and pepper to taste
2 t. dried oregano
1/4 t. red pepper flakes

salt and pepper to taste
1 c. elbow macaroni, cooked
2 c. whipping cream
1/4 c. fresh Italian parsley, chopped
Garnish: shredded mozzarella cheese, grated Parmesan cheese

Heat oil in a large skillet over medium heat. Brown sausage in oil; drain. Stir in pepperoni and salami; cook for one to 2 minutes. Add green pepper, onion and garlic to sausage mixture; cook for about 5 minutes, until vegetables have softened. Stir in flour. Spoon sausage mixture into a slow cooker. Add tomatoes with juice, broth and seasonings to slow cooker. Cover and cook on low setting for 3 to 4 hours, until vegetables are tender and soup has thickened. About 20 minutes before serving, stir in cooked pasta, cream and parsley. Garnish servings with cheeses. Serves 6 to 8.

Chicken-Corn Soup

Nichole Sullivan, Santa Fe, TX

2 to 3 potatoes, peeled and diced
3 carrots, peeled and diced
2 stalks celery, diced
1/2 onion, diced
1 T. garlic, minced
1 to 2 lbs. boneless, skinless chicken breasts, diced
1 to 2 t. Italian seasoning
salt and pepper to taste
14-3/4 oz. can creamed corn
14-1/4 oz. can corn, drained
6-oz. can tomato paste
3 c. chicken broth
1/4 c. fresh cilantro, chopped

In a large slow cooker, layer potatoes, carrots, celery, onion and garlic. Add chicken, seasonings, both cans of corn and tomato paste. Top with broth and cilantro. Cover and cook on low setting for 8 to 9 hours, or on high setting for 4 to 5 hours. Makes 8 to 10 servings.

Game-Day Corn Chowder

Jo Ann

1 lb. smoked pork sausage, diced
3 c. frozen hashbrowns with onions and peppers
2 carrots, peeled and chopped
15-oz. can creamed corn
10-3/4 oz. can cream of mushroom soup with roasted garlic
2 c. water

Brown sausage in a skillet over medium heat; drain. Place sausage in a slow cooker; top with hashbrowns and carrots. Combine corn, soup and water; stir until blended and pour over sausage mixture. Cover and cook on low setting for 8 to 10 hours. Serves 6.

Snow-Day Potato Soup

Susann Minall-Hunter, Spring Hill, FL

6 potatoes, peeled and diced
2 leeks, chopped
2 onions, chopped
1 carrot, peeled and thinly sliced
4 c. water
1/2 t. pepper
4 cubes chicken bouillon
2 10-3/4 oz. cans cream of mushroom soup
1 T. dried parsley
2 T. butter
12-oz. can evaporated milk
Garnish: chopped fresh chives

Combine all ingredients except evaporated milk and garnish in a large slow cooker. Cover and cook on low setting for 8 to 10 hours, or on high setting for 3 to 4 hours. Stir in milk during the last hour. Serve garnished with chives. Makes 6 servings.

Game-Day Corn Chowder

Quick tip

To skim fat from a pot of soup, lay a slice of bread on top for just a few minutes

Mom's Black-Eyed Pea Soup

Mom's Black-Eyed Pea Soup

Dana Cunningham Lafayette, LA

16-oz. pkg. dried
  black-eyed peas
10-3/4 oz. can bean with
  bacon soup
4 c. water
6 carrots, peeled and
  chopped
2-lb. beef chuck roast,
  cubed
1/4 t. pepper

Combine dried peas and remaining ingredients in a slow cooker; mix well. Cover and cook on low setting for 9 to 10 hours. Makes 6 servings.

Mamma Mia's Italian Stew

Connie Bryan, Topeka, KS

1 lb. ground hot Italian
  sausage, browned and
  drained
1 eggplant, peeled and
  cubed
1-1/2 c. green beans,
  sliced
2 green peppers, sliced
1 to 2 potatoes, peeled
  and cubed
1 zucchini, cubed
1 yellow squash, cubed
1 c. onion, thinly sliced
15-oz. can Italian-style
  tomato sauce
1/4 c. olive oil
2 t. garlic, minced
1 t. salt

Combine all ingredients in a slow cooker; mix well. Cover and cook on low setting for 8 hours, or on high setting for 4 hours. Makes 8 to 10 servings.

Best Cabbage Soup

Rebecca Wright, Tulsa, OK

16-oz. pkg. smoked pork
  sausage, cut into 1-inch
  pieces
28-oz. can diced
  tomatoes
1/2 head cabbage, thinly
  sliced
2 carrots, peeled and
  chopped
2 stalks celery, chopped
2 potatoes, peeled and
  chopped
2 14-1/2 oz. cans
  chicken broth
20-oz. can vegetable
  cocktail juice
1 onion, chopped
1 T. garlic, minced
1 T. ground cumin
1-1/2 t. dried oregano
1-1/2 c. shredded
  Monterey Jack cheese

In a large slow cooker, combine sausage, undrained tomatoes and vegetables. Add broth and juice. Cover and cook on low setting for 6 to 8 hours, or on high setting for 3 hours, until vegetables are tender. Makes 6 servings.

Santa Fe Corn & Bean Soup

Athena Colegrove, Big Springs, TX

1 lb. ground beef
1/2 onion, diced
2 10-oz. can diced tomatoes with green-chiles
2 c. water
16-oz. can kidney beans
16-oz. can pinto beans
16-oz. can black beans
11-oz. can corn
1-oz. pkg. ranch salad dressing mix
1-1/4 oz. pkg. taco seasoning mix

Brown beef and onion together in a skillet; drain. Transfer to a slow cooker; mix in remaining ingredients. Do not drain vegetables. Cover and cook on low setting for 6 to 8 hours, or on high setting for 3 to 4 hours, until heated through. Serves 6 to 8.

Ellen's Tortilla Soup

Sharon Buxton, Warsaw, OH

4 boneless, skinless chicken breasts, or 4 c. cooked turkey, cubed
2 10-oz. cans diced tomatoes and chiles with lime juice & cilantro
4-oz. can chopped green chiles
15-1/2 oz. can black beans, drained and rinsed
15-oz. can tomato sauce
1 c. salsa
Garnish: sour cream, shredded Cheddar cheese, tortilla chips

Place chicken or turkey in a large slow cooker. Add undrained tomatoes, undrained chiles, beans, tomato sauce and salsa. Cover and cook on low setting for about 8 hours. If using chicken breasts, during last 2 hours remove chicken and shred; return to crock. Serve individual bowls garnished with sour cream, cheese and tortilla chips. Makes 8 to 10 servings.

Slow-Cooker Irish Stew

Amy Shilliday, Tampa, FL

1/2 c. all-purpose flour
1 T. salt
1 t. cracked pepper
1 to 2 lbs. stew beef or lamb, cubed
2 T. lard or shortening
3 potatoes, peeled and diced
2 carrots, peeled and diced
1-oz. pkg. beefy onion soup mix
2 10-oz. cans beef gravy
1 c. Irish stout or beef broth
additional salt and pepper to taste

Combine flour, salt and pepper in a large plastic zipping bag. Add meat; shake to coat. Place coated meat in a colander and shake over the sink to remove excess flour. Melt lard or shortening in skillet over medium-high heat. Brown meat in skillet; drain. Add meat and remaining ingredients to a slow cooker. Cover and cook on low setting for 6 to 8 hours, or until meat and vegetables are tender. Serves 6 to 8.

Slow-Cooker Irish Stew

Quick tip

Keep a container in the freezer for leftover veggies, then make a big pot of vegetable soup. Thaw and place in a slow cooker. Add water to cover, seasonings and a can of tomato sauce. Cover and cook on low all day...delicious!

Smoky Sausage & 2-Bean Soup

Smoky Sausage & 2-Bean Soup

Rebecca Ross, Topeka, KS

1 lb. smoked pork sausage, sliced

15-oz. can tomato sauce

2 14-1/2 oz. cans low-sodium beef broth

15-oz. can pinto beans, drained and rinsed

15-oz. can kidney beans, drained and rinsed

1/4 c. onion, chopped

1/4 c. celery, chopped

1/4 c. green pepper, chopped

1/4 c. red pepper, chopped

1 c. water

2 cubes beef bouillon

1/2 t. pepper

1/4 t. garlic salt

1/2 t. Italian seasoning

1 to 2 c. cooked rice

Combine all ingredients except rice in a slow cooker. Cover and cook on low setting for 6 to 8 hours. About 30 minutes before serving, stir in rice. Cover and cook for remaining 30 minutes. Makes 8 to 10 servings.

Spuds & Sausage Stew

Sue Gehr, Lititz, PA

1 lb. smoked pork sausage, sliced 3/4-inch thick

5 redskin potatoes, cut in 1-inch cubes

4 carrots, peeled and cut in 3/4-inch slices

10-3/4 oz. can cream of mushroom soup

Optional: 1 onion, sliced

Combine all ingredients in a slow cooker. Cover and cook on low setting for 6 to 8 hours. Makes 4 servings.

Lazy-Day Soup

Kimberly Wacht, Tuba City, AZ

28-oz. pkg. frozen diced potatoes with onion and peppers

3 14-1/2 oz. cans chicken broth

16-oz. jar pasteurized process cheese sauce

10-3/4 oz. can cream of celery soup

1 to 2 c. cooked ham or Polish sausage, diced

Mix together all ingredients in slow cooker. Cover and cook on low setting for 6 to 8 hours, or on high setting for 3 hours. Serves 4 to 6.

Down-on-the-Bayou Gumbo

Sue Neely, Greenville, IL

3 T. all-purpose flour
3 T. oil
3 c. chicken broth
1/2 lb. smoked pork sausage,
  sliced

2 c. frozen okra
14-1/2 oz. can diced tomatoes
1 onion, chopped
1 green pepper, chopped
3 cloves garlic, minced

1/4 t. cayenne pepper
3/4 lb. cooked medium shrimp,
  cleaned and tails removed
cooked rice

Stir together flour and oil in a saucepan over medium heat. Cook, stirring constantly, for 5 minutes. Reduce heat; cook and stir for 10 minutes, until mixture is reddish brown. Pour broth into a slow cooker; stir in flour mixture. Add remaining ingredients except shrimp and rice. Cover and cook on low setting for 7 to 9 hours. Shortly before serving, add shrimp to slow cooker; mix well. Cover and cook on low setting for about 20 minutes. Ladle gumbo over cooked rice in soup bowls. Serves 6.

Creamy Potato Soup

Roberta Simpkins, Mentor-on-the-Lake, OH

6 potatoes, peeled and cubed
2 onions, chopped
1 carrot, sliced
1 stalk celery, sliced

4 cubes chicken bouillon
1 T. dried parsley
5 c. water
1/4 t. pepper

1 T. salt
1/3 c. butter, melted
12-oz. can evaporated milk

Combine all ingredients except evaporated milk in a slow cooker. Cover and cook on low setting for 10 to 12 hours, or on high setting for 3 to 4 hours. Stir in milk during last hour of cooking. Serves 6.

Down-on-the-Bayou Gumbo

Quick tip

Homemade croutons add a special touch to soup. Cut shapes from day-old bread using mini cookie cutters. Spread with a little softened butter, sprinkle with garlic powder and bake at 350 degrees for just a few minutes, until crisp.

Quick tip

Turn mini pumpkins into candle holders by cutting out the center and placing a taper inside. Candles in terra cotta pots also add to the natural look of harvest-time.

Pumpkin White Chili

Pumpkin White Chili

Rachel Boyd, Defiance, OH

28-oz. can chicken
32-oz. jar Great Northern beans
1 pie pumpkin, peeled, seeded
  and cubed
1 sweet potato, peeled and
  chopped
1/2 c. pearl onions
5 cloves garlic, minced
2 t. dried parsley
1 t. dried rosemary
1 t. cinnamon

Combine undrained chicken, undrained beans and remaining ingredients in a slow cooker. Cover and cook on high setting for 5 hours, or until pumpkin and potatoes are tender. Serves 6 to 8.

Beer-Braised Pork & Black Bean Soup

Michelle Vandergrift, Drayden, MD

2 12-oz. bottles regular or
  non-alcoholic beer
1 T. chipotle chiles in adobo sauce,
  chopped
1 T. reserved adobo sauce
1 T. red wine vinegar
1 T. hot pepper sauce
1 t. ground cumin
1 onion, chopped
1 lb. dried black beans
1-1/2 lb. boneless pork butt
  shoulder roast
salt and pepper to taste
cooked rice
Garnish: salsa, sour cream,
  chopped fresh cilantro

Combine all ingredients except rice and garnish in a slow cooker; mix well. Cover and cook on high setting for 4-1/2 to 5 hours, until pork is very tender. Shred pork in soup using 2 forks; stir. Divide rice among soup bowls; ladle soup over rice. Garnish servings with salsa, sour cream and cilantro. Serves 6 to 8.

Mom's Shredded BBQ

Lori Drew, Ely, NV

2-lb. beef roast, cubed
1 onion, coarsely chopped
1 green or red pepper, coarsely chopped
18-oz. bottle favorite barbecue sauce
1/4 to 1/2 c. water
4 to 6 hard rolls or hamburger buns, split
Garnish: sliced red onion, dill pickles

Place beef in a slow cooker; top with vegetables, barbecue sauce and water. Cover and cook on low setting for 6 to 8 hours, until beef shreds easily. Using 2 forks, shred beef and return to slow cooker to keep warm. Serve on rolls or buns, topped with slices of red onion and dill pickles. Makes 4 to 6 sandwiches.

French Dips on a Budget

Cheryl Sullivan, Winfield, IA

3 to 4-lb. beef rump roast
1/2 c. soy sauce
1.35-oz. pkg. onion soup mix
salt and pepper to taste
3 to 4 c. water
8 to 10 sandwich rolls, split

Place roast in a slow cooker. Drizzle with soy sauce; sprinkle with soup mix, salt and pepper. Add enough water to cover roast. Cover and cook on low setting for 10 hours, or until beef is very tender. Remove beef from slow cooker and slice or shred. To serve, place beef on rolls for sandwiches; serve with juices from slow cooker for dipping. Serves 8 to 10.

Virginia-Style Beef Sandwiches

Ursula Juarez-Wall, Dumfries, VA

2-1/2 to 3-lb. beef round or shoulder roast
1 c. catsup
12-oz. can beer or non-alcoholic beer
1-1/2 oz. pkg. onion soup mix
8 hamburger buns, split
Garnish: bottled barbecue sauce

Place roast in a slow cooker; set aside. Mix together catsup, beer and soup mix in a bowl; pour over roast. Cover and cook on low setting for 4 to 4-1/2 hours. Shred roast with 2 forks. Spoon shredded beef onto buns and serve topped with barbecue sauce. Makes 8 sandwiches.

French Dips on a Budget

Irish Corned Beef Dinner

Quick tip

National Sandwich Day is
November 3rd...celebrate
and serve up a favorite sandwich!

Irish Corned Beef Dinner

Lisanne Miller, Canton, MS

3-lb. corned beef brisket

4 to 6 potatoes, quartered

1 lb. carrots, peeled, halved and
cut into sticks

1 head cabbage, cut into wedges

2 onions, quartered

12-oz. can beer or non-alcoholic
beer

1 bay leaf

2 to 3 c. water

Place corned beef in a slow cooker. Arrange vegetables around brisket; add beer, bay leaf and enough water to cover. Cover and cook on low setting for 7 to 8 hours. Discard bay leaf. To serve, arrange vegetables on a large serving platter. Slice brisket and arrange over vegetables. Makes 6 servings.

New England Dinner

Cinda Rogers, Buhler, KS

2 carrots, peeled and sliced

1 onion, sliced

2 stalks celery, sliced

3 to 4-lb. boneless beef chuck
roast

1 t. salt

1 t. pepper

1.35 -oz. pkg onion soup mix

2 c. water

1 cabbage, cut into wedges

3 T. butter

2 T. all-purpose flour

Combine carrots, onion and celery in a large slow cooker. Place roast on top of carrot mixture; sprinkle with salt, pepper and soup mix. Drizzle water over all. Cover and cook on low setting 8 to 9 hours. Increase heat to high setting; add cabbage. Cover and cook for another 45 to 50 minutes. Meanwhile, melt butter in a saucepan over medium heat. Whisk flour into melted butter until smooth; add 1/2 to 2 cups broth from slow cooker. Cook gravy, stirring constantly, until smooth. Serve beef and vegetables with gravy. Serves 4 to 6.

Italian Beef & Pasta

Evelyn Webb, Chicago Heights, IL

3 to 4-lb. beef chuck roast
2 onions, sliced
13-1/4 oz. can sliced mushrooms

2 26-oz. jars marinara pasta sauce
2 T. zesty Italian salad dressing
  mix

16-oz. pkg. spaghetti, cooked

Combine all ingredients except spaghetti in a slow cooker. Cover and cook on low setting for 8 hours. Slice beef; spoon sauce over cooked pasta and serve beef on the side. Serves 8 to 10.

Best-Ever Lasagna

Cherylann Smith, Efland, NC

1 lb. ground beef, browned and
  drained
1 t. Italian seasoning
8 lasagna noodles, uncooked and
  broken into thirds

28-oz. jar spaghetti sauce
1/3 c. water
4-oz. can sliced mushrooms,
  drained
15-oz. container ricotta cheese

8-oz. pkg. shredded mozzarella
  cheese
Garnish: shredded Parmesan
  cheese

Combine ground beef and Italian seasoning. Arrange half of the lasagna noodles in a greased slow cooker. Spread half of the ground beef mixture over noodles. Top with half each of remaining ingredients except Parmesan cheese. Repeat layering process. Cover and cook on low setting for 5 hours. Garnish with Parmesan cheese. Serves 10.

Hearty Italian Sandwiches

Kristie Rigo, Friedens, PA

1 lb. ground beef
1 lb. ground Italian sausage
1 onion, chopped
1 green pepper, chopped

1 red pepper, chopped
1 t. salt
1 t. pepper
1/2 t. red pepper flakes

3/4 c. Italian salad dressing
12 sandwich rolls, split
12 slices provolone cheese

Brown ground beef and sausage together in a skillet; drain and set aside. Place one-third of onion and peppers in a slow cooker; top with half of meat mixture. Repeat layers with remaining vegetables and meat. Sprinkle with salt, pepper and red pepper flakes; pour salad dressing over top. Cover and cook on low setting for 6 hours. Serve on rolls, topped with cheese. Makes 12 sandwiches.

Best-Ever Lasagna

Quick tip

If it's a warm spring or summer day, consider enjoying dinner outside...Italian style! Set the table with touches of green, white and red... the colors of the Italian flag are ideal paired with bunches of grapes and Italian music playing in the background.

Beefy Mushroom Bake

Beefy Mushroom Casserole

Claire Bertram, Lexington, KY

1 to 1-1/2 lbs. beef round
  steak, cubed
3/4 c. quick-cooking barley,
  uncooked
10-3/4 oz. can golden

mushroom soup
2/3 c. water
3/4 lb. sliced mushrooms
Garnish: shredded cheese,
  diced green onions

Combine all ingredients in a slow cooker; mix well.
Cover and cook on low setting for 7 to 8 hours. Garnish
as desired. Serves 4 to 6.

Beef Tips & Gravy

Kathleen White, Cato, NY

3 lbs. stew beef, cubed
15-oz. can tomato sauce
2 c. water
1.35-oz. pkg. onion soup
  mix

1/3 c. instant tapioca,
  uncooked
1 to 2 t. beef bouillon
  granules
cooked egg noodles

Place beef in a slow cooker. Combine remaining
ingredients except noodles; pour over beef. Cover
and cook on low setting for 8 to 10 hours, or on high
setting for 5 to 6 hours. Serve over cooked noodles.
Serves 6 to 8.

French Onion Beef

Dawn Dodge, Roscommon, MI

1-1/4 lbs. boneless beef
  round steak, cut into
  6 pieces
8-oz. pkg. sliced
  mushrooms
1 c. onion, sliced and
  separated into rings

10-3/4 oz. can French
  onion soup
6-1/4 oz. pkg. herb-
  flavored stuffing mix
1/4 c. butter, melted
8-oz. pkg. shredded
  mozzarella cheese

Layer half of beef, mushrooms and onion in a slow
cooker; repeat layers. Pour soup over top; cover and cook
on low setting for 8 to 10 hours. Shortly before serving,
toss stuffing mix with its seasoning packet, melted butter
and 1/2 cup liquid from slow cooker. Spread stuffing
mixture on top of beef. Increase to high setting; cover
and cook for 10 minutes, or until stuffing is fluffy.
Sprinkle with cheese; cover and heat until cheese is
melted. Serves 4 to 6.

Savory Merlot Pot Roast

Heather McClintock, Columbus, OH

3 to 4-lb. beef chuck roast
1/2 t. meat tenderizer
pepper to taste
1 t. olive oil
10-3/4 oz. can cream of
  mushroom soup

1-1/2 oz. pkg. onion soup
  mix
1/2 c. merlot wine or beef
  broth
Optional: 1 T. cornstarch,
  2 T. cold water

Sprinkle roast on all sides with tenderizer and pepper. Heat oil over medium heat in a large non-stick skillet. Brown roast on all sides and transfer to a slow cooker. Combine soup, soup mix and wine or broth; pour over roast. Cover and cook on low setting for 6 to 8 hours. Remove roast to a serving platter; cover with aluminum foil to keep warm. If thicker gravy is desired, increase setting to high; mix cornstarch into water and stir into gravy in slow cooker. Cook, uncovered, for 10 to 20 minutes, until gravy reaches desired thickness. Serve gravy with roast. Serves 6 to 8.

Paprika Beef & Noodles

Teresa Pearman, Marshall, NC

1-3/4 c. water, divided
2 lbs. stew beef cubes
1 c. onion, sliced
1 clove garlic, diced
3/4 c. catsup
2 T. Worcestershire sauce
1 T. brown sugar, packed

2 t. salt
2 t. paprika
1/8 t. dry mustard
1/8 t. cayenne pepper
2 T. all-purpose flour
cooked egg noodles

In a slow cooker, combine 1-1/2 cups water and remaining ingredients except flour and noodles; mix well. Cover and cook on low setting for 6 to 8 hours. In a cup, stir together remaining water and flour. Drizzle into beef mixture; stir. Cook, uncovered, until thickened. Serve beef mixture over noodles. Serves 6 to 8.

Smoky Beef Brisket

Rita Morgan, Pueblo, CO

2-1/2 lb. beef brisket,
  halved
1 T. smoke-flavored
  cooking sauce
1 t. salt

1/2 t. pepper
1/2 c. onion, chopped
1/2 c. catsup
2 t. Dijon mustard
1/2 t. celery seed

Rub brisket with smoke-flavored cooking sauce, salt and pepper; place in a slow cooker. Top with onion. Combine remaining ingredients; spread over brisket. Cover and cook on low setting for 8 to 9 hours. Remove brisket and keep warm. Transfer cooking juices to a blender; process until smooth. Serve with brisket. Serves 4 to 6.

Quick tip

Garnishes make slow-cooked foods look extra delicious! Sprinkle on diced red peppers, minced chives or shredded cheese just before serving.

Paprika Beef & Noodles

Quick tip

For flavorful, fast-fix bread to serve with dinner, simply brush Italian bread slices with butter. Sprinkle on garlic & herb seasoning blend and broil until golden.

Bowtie Lasagna Casserole

Bowtie Lasagna Casserole

Kristi Magowan, Greenwich, NY

1 lb. ground beef
1 T. olive oil
1 onion, chopped
2 t. garlic, chopped
28-oz. can crushed
  tomatoes
8-oz. can tomato sauce
1 T. brown sugar, packed
1 T. dried oregano

salt and pepper to taste
8-oz. pkg. bowtie pasta,
  uncooked
15-oz. container ricotta
  cheese
1 c. shredded mozzarella
  cheese
Garnish: grated
  Parmesan cheese

In a skillet over medium heat, cook beef until no longer pink. Drain; add to a slow cooker. Add olive oil and onion to skillet; cook until translucent, 5 to 7 minutes. Add garlic; cook for one minute. Spoon onion mixture over beef; stir in undrained tomatoes, tomato sauce, brown sugar and seasonings. Cover and cook on low setting for 6 to 7 hours. About 30 minutes before serving, cook pasta according to package directions; drain. Add cooked pasta and ricotta cheese to sauce in slow cooker; stir to combine. Top with mozzarella cheese. Turn slow cooker to high setting. Cover and cook for an additional 30 minutes, until heated through and cheese is melted. Serve garnished with Parmesan cheese. Makes 8 to 12 servings.

Spaghetti & Meatballs

Susie Backus, Delaware, OH

1 lb. frozen cooked
  meatballs, thawed
26-oz. jar spaghetti sauce
1 onion, chopped
1-1/2 c. water

8-oz. pkg. spaghetti,
  uncooked and broken
  into 3-inch pieces
Garnish: grated
  Parmesan cheese

Combine meatballs, spaghetti sauce, onion and water in a slow cooker. Cover and cook on low setting for 6 to 8 hours. Stir well; add broken spaghetti. Increase to high setting; cover and cook for an additional hour, stirring once during cooking. Serve with Parmesan cheese. Serves 4 to 6.

Busy-Day Spinach Lasagna

Teresa Eller, Tonganoxie, KS

2 lbs. extra-lean ground
  beef
2 T. Italian seasoning,
  divided
2 14-1/2 oz. cans diced
  tomatoes, divided
2 8-oz. cans tomato sauce,
  divided

6 c. fresh spinach, torn and
  divided
3 c. shredded Swiss or
  mozzarella cheese,
  divided
12-oz. pkg. lasagna
  noodles, uncooked and
  broken up

Break up uncooked beef and place in a slow cooker sprayed with non-stick vegetable spray. Sprinkle beef with one tablespoon Italian seasoning. Add one can tomatoes with juice and one can tomato sauce; stir gently to combine. Add half of spinach; press down gently. Add one cup cheese and half of uncooked noodles. Repeat layers, ending with cheese on top. Cover and cook on low setting for 8 hours. Makes 6 to 8 servings.

Party Joes

Julie Dawson, Prospect Heights, IL

3 lbs. ground beef
2 c. onion, chopped
2 15-oz. cans tomato sauce
12-oz. jar chili sauce

1/2 c. steak sauce
1 T. garlic, chopped
10 to 12 onion sandwich rolls, split

Brown beef and onion in a skillet over medium heat; drain. Spoon beef mixture into a slow cooker. Stir sauces and garlic into beef mixture. Cover and cook on low setting for 2 to 3 hours, until heated through. Serve on rolls for sandwiches. Serves 10 to 12.

Classic Coney Sauce

Cathy Young, Evansville, IN

3 lbs. lean ground beef, browned
  and drained
28-oz. can tomato purée
1 c. onion, chopped

2 T. chili powder
1-1/2 T. mustard
1-1/2 T. Worcestershire sauce
1 T. salt

1 T. pepper
1 t. garlic powder

Combine all ingredients in a slow cooker. Cover and cook on high setting for 3 hours, stirring occasionally. Turn heat to low setting to keep warm. Makes enough sauce for about 20 hot dogs.

Aunt Betty's Sloppy Joes

Laurie Campbell, Madison, WI

3 lbs. ground beef
1 c. onion, chopped
1 c. red pepper, chopped
3 cloves garlic, chopped

1 carrot, peeled and finely
  shredded
1-1/2 c. catsup
1/2 c. water

1/4 c. spicy mustard
1/4 c. cider vinegar
3 T. Worcestershire sauce
10 hamburger buns, split

In a skillet over medium heat, cook ground beef, onion, pepper and garlic until browned and tender; drain. Combine in a slow cooker with remaining ingredients except buns. Cover and cook on low setting for 6 to 8 hours, or on high setting for 3 to 4 hours. Spoon onto buns. Makes 10 sandwiches.

Classic Coney Sauce

Quick tip

When cooking veggies with pot roast, add them halfway through cooking time for a firmer texture.

Pepperoncini Italian Beef Roast

Pepperoncini Italian Beef Roast

Vickie

4-lb. beef chuck roast

8-oz. jar pepperoncini peppers, drained and juice reserved

1 onion, sliced

2 1-oz. pkgs. au jus mix

8 to 10 hoagie rolls, split

Place roast in a slow cooker; pour reserved pepper juice over top. Cover and cook on low setting for 6 to 8 hours, until very tender. Remove roast and shred with 2 forks; stir back into liquid in slow cooker. Add peppers and onion. Blend au jus mix with a little of the liquid from slow cooker until dissolved. Pour over beef; add water if needed to cover roast. Cover and cook for an additional hour. Serve beef spooned onto rolls. Serves 8 to 10.

Louisiana-Style Pot Roast

Teri Naquin, Melville, LA

4-lb. beef chuck roast

salt and pepper to taste

2 T. oil

1.35-oz. pkg. onion soup mix

1 onion, chopped

1 c. water

3 carrots, peeled and chopped

3 potatoes, peeled and cubed

Optional: 1 stalk celery, chopped

Sprinkle roast with salt and pepper. In a large skillet over medium-high heat, brown roast in oil on all sides; place in a slow cooker. Add remaining ingredients. Cover and cook on low setting for 8 to 10 hours. Makes 8 to 10 servings.

Cola Roast

Wendy Hall, East Canton, OH

3-lb. beef pot roast

1.35-oz. pkg. onion soup mix

2 12-oz. cans cola

Place roast in a slow cooker; sprinkle with soup mix. Pour cola over top. Cover and cook on low setting for 7 to 8 hours. Makes 8 to 10 servings.

So-Easy Slow-Cooker Pot Roast
Hilary Stubblebine, Delaware, OH

3 to 4-lb. beef chuck roast
10-3/4 oz. can tomato soup
10-3/4 oz. can cream of
  mushroom soup

2 16-oz. cans new
  potatoes, drained
2 14-1/2 oz. cans sliced
  carrots, drained

Mix together all ingredients in a slow cooker. Cover and cook on low setting for 7 to 8 hours. Serves 6.

Sunday Beef & Noodles
Peggy Donnally, Toledo, OH

2-lb. beef chuck roast
4 c. beef broth
1 c. onion, chopped
2 t. onion powder
1 t. garlic powder

1 T. dried parsley
salt and pepper to taste
16-oz. pkg. extra-wide
  egg noodles, cooked
mashed potatoes

Place roast in a slow cooker. Combine broth, onion and seasonings; pour over roast. Cover and cook on low setting for 6 to 8 hours. Remove roast; slice and return to slow cooker. Add noodles to slow cooker; heat through. Serve over mashed potatoes. Serves 6.

Glazed Carrots
Bruce Burton, Galena, OH

16-oz. pkg. baby carrots
1/2 c. orange juice
5 T. brown sugar, packed

2 T. butter
1/8 t. salt
1/8 t. pepper

Cover carrots with water in a saucepan. Cook until tender; drain. Add juice to saucepan; simmer until almost evaporated. Stir in remaining ingredients; cook until well blended and glazed. Serves 6.

Quick tip

Remember that long, slow cooking is ideal for inexpensive cuts of meat because it provides plenty of time for tenderizing.

Sunday Beef & Noodles

Easy Roast Beef Sandwiches

Easy Roast Beef Sandwiches

Cynthia Holtz, Park Forest, IL

4 to 5-lb. beef chuck
   roast
0.7-oz. pkg. Italian salad
   dressing mix
8 to 10 pepperoncini
   peppers

2 c. water
16 to 20 sandwich buns
Garnish: brown mustard,
   roasted red pepper
   strips

Add beef, salad dressing mix and peppers to slow cooker: pour in water. Cover and cook on low setting for 10 hours. Remove beef from slow cooker and shred; return shredded beef to juices in slow cooker. Serve shredded beef on buns; top with mustard and roasted red pepper strips. Makes 16 to 20 sandwiches.

Jenny's BBQ Beef Sandwiches

Jenny Bishoff, Swanton, MD

2 lbs. stew beef, cubed
18-oz. bottle barbecue
   sauce

12-oz. can cola
6 to 8 sandwich buns,
   split

Mix together all ingredients except buns in slow cooker. Cover and cook on low setting for 6 to 8 hours. Serve on buns. Makes 6 to 8 sandwiches

Chicago-Style Italian Beef Sandwiches

Sandra Sullivan, Aurora, CO

3-lb. boneless beef chuck
   roast
4 t. garlic pepper
1 T. oil
14-1/2 oz. can beef broth
0.7-oz. pkg. Italian salad
   dressing mix
1 t. onion salt
1 t. dried oregano

1 t. dried basil
1 t. dried parsley
16-oz. jar pepperoncini
   peppers, drained
8 hoagie buns, split and
   toasted
2 c. shredded provolone
   cheese

Trim fat from roast. Season roast on all sides with garlic pepper. Heat oil in a skillet over medium heat; brown roast on all sides in oil. Transfer roast to a slow cooker. Add broth, dressing mix and seasonings to roast. Mix well; top with peppers. Cover and cook on low setting for 10 hours. Remove roast from slow cooker; shred and set aside. Remove peppers from slow cooker with a slotted spoon; place in a small bowl and set aside. Ladle juices from slow cooker into small bowls. Serve beef on buns, topped with peppers and cheese, with bowls of juices for dipping. Serves 8.

Honey-Mustard Short Ribs

David Wink, Gooseberry Patch

3 to 4 lbs. bone-in beef short ribs
salt and pepper to taste
1 c. hickory smoke-flavored
   barbecue sauce

3 T. honey
1 T. Dijon mustard
3 cloves garlic, minced

2 T. cornstarch
2 T. cold water

Sprinkle ribs with salt and pepper; place in a slow cooker and set aside. Combine honey, barbecue sauce, mustard, garlic and additional salt and pepper, if desired; pour over ribs. Cover and cook on low setting for 6 to 7 hours. During the last 30 minutes of cooking, whisk cornstarch into water; add to slow cooker, stirring until thickened. Serves 4.

Orange & Ginger Beef Short Ribs

Lee Beedle, Martinsburg, WV

1/3 c. soy sauce
3 T. brown sugar, packed
3 T. white vinegar
2 cloves garlic, minced

1/2 t. chili powder
1 T. fresh ginger, peeled and
   minced

3 lbs. boneless beef short ribs
1/3 c. orange marmalade

In a large plastic zipping bag, combine all ingredients except ribs and marmalade. Add ribs to bag; turn to coat well. Refrigerate at least 2 hours to overnight. Drain ribs, reserving marinade. Place ribs in a slow cooker. Add marmalade to reserved marinade; mix well and pour over ribs. Cover and cook on low setting for 6 to 8 hours. Serves 6.

Orange & Ginger Beef Short Ribs

Quick tip

Make a scrapbook of Mom's favorite recipes...just going through the recipe box together. Choose favorite recipes, make copies and add family photos. Taken to the nearest copy shop, extras of the scrapbook can quickly and easily be made to share with family & friends.

Hearty Hominy Beef Stew

🍴 Quick side

When time is short, a super-fast dessert is in order. Fill sundae cups with cubes of angel food cake layered with pie filling!

Hearty Hominy Beef Stew,

Rita Morgan, Pueblo, CO

1 onion, chopped
2-lb. beef chuck roast, cubed
1/4 t. salt
1 green pepper, chopped
3 carrots, peeled and sliced

3 stalks celery, sliced
3 cloves garlic, minced
14-1/2 oz. can petite diced
　tomatoes
1 c. beef broth, divided

2 T. cornstarch
15-oz. can hominy, drained and
　rinsed

Place onion in a lightly greased slow cooker; top with beef. Sprinkle with salt. Add green pepper, carrots, celery and garlic to slow cooker. Pour tomatoes with juice and 3/4 cup broth over all. Cover and cook on low setting for 8 hours. In a bowl, mix together cornstarch and remaining broth until smooth; stir into slow cooker during the last 15 minutes of cooking. Stir in hominy and heat through. Serves 6.

Slow-Cooker Cheesesteak Sandwiches

Kristy Still, Broken Arrow, OK

1 lb. beef round steak, thinly sliced
1/2 onion, diced
1 red pepper, diced
1-1/2 t. garlic powder

1 T. butter
1 T. Worcestershire sauce
1 cube beef bouillon

16-oz. pkg. shredded Colby Jack
　cheese
4 hoagie rolls, split

Add all ingredients except cheese and rolls to a lightly greased slow cooker. Pour in enough water to just cover the ingredients. Cover and cook on low setting for 6 to 8 hours. Using a slotted spoon, place a serving of steak mixture on the bottom of each roll; sprinkle with cheese. Replace tops of rolls to make sandwiches. Makes 4 sandwiches.

Beef It Up

Fiesta Beef Enchiladas

Jane Terrill, Cookson, OK

1 to 2 lbs. ground beef, browned and drained
1 onion, chopped
10-oz. can mild enchilada sauce
4-oz. can diced green chiles
2 10-3/4 oz. cans Cheddar cheese soup
10-3/4 oz. can cream of chicken soup
10-3/4 oz. can cream of mushroom soup
12 6-inch corn tortillas, torn into bite-size pieces

Combine all ingredients except tortillas in a slow cooker; mix well. Cover and cook on low setting for 8 to 10 hours, or on high setting for 4 hours. Stir in tortillas one hour before serving time. Serves 6.

Slow-Cooker Enchiladas

Panda Spurgin, Berryville, AK

1 lb. ground beef
1 c. onion, chopped
1/2 c. green pepper, chopped
15-1/2 oz. can black beans, drained and rinsed
10-oz. can diced tomatoes with green chiles
1/3 c. water
1 t. chili powder
1/2 t. ground cumin
1/2 t. salt
1/4 t. pepper
2 to 3 c. shredded Monterey Jack cheese
6 flour tortillas
Garnish: salsa, sour cream

In a skillet over medium heat, brown beef, onion and pepper; drain. Stir in remaining ingredients except cheese, tortillas and garnish; bring to a simmer. Cook stirring occasionally until heated through, about 5 minutes. In a slow cooker, alternate layers of beef mixture, tortillas and cheese, ending with cheese. Cover and cook on low setting for 5 to 7 hours. Garnish servings as desired. Serves 6.

Mexicali Beef Soft Tacos

Kathy Lowe, Orem, UT

1/2 to 1 c. water
4 to 5-lb. beef chuck roast
1/2 red onion, chopped
3 cloves garlic
1/4 c. oil
1 T. red pepper flakes
2 t. ground cumin
2 t. dried oregano
1 t. pepper
10 to 12 10-inch flour tortillas, warmed
Garnish: lettuce, chopped onion, chopped tomatoes, sour cream, salsa

Pour water into a slow cooker; add roast and set aside. Combine onion, garlic, oil and seasonings in a blender. Blend until mixed; pour over roast. Cover and cook on high setting for about 7 hours, until roast is very tender. Shred roast with 2 forks; return to slow cooker. Cover and cook on low setting for an additional hour. Fill tortillas with beef mixture; add toppings as desired. Makes 10 to 12 servings.

Mexicali Beef Soft Tacos

Quick tip

Try something new...onion buns topped with Saucy Hamburgers taste great!

All-American Cheeseburgers

All-American Cheeseburgers

Claire Bertram, Lexington, KY

1 lb. ground beef, browned
  and drained
3 T. catsup
2 t. mustard

2 c. pasteurized process
  cheese spread, cubed
10 hamburger buns, split

Place ground beef in a slow cooker; add catsup and mustard, mixing well. Top with cubed cheese. Cover and cook on low setting for 3 to 4 hours. Stir beef mixture gently; spoon onto buns. Makes 10 sandwiches.

Saucy Hamburgers

Jennifer Kann, Dayton, OH

1-1/2 lbs. ground beef
1 onion, sliced into rings
1 c. catsup
1/2 to 3/4 c. water

2 T. butter, melted
2 T. sugar
salt and pepper to taste
6 hamburger buns, split

Form ground beef into 6 patties. Brown in a skillet over medium heat; drain. Combine remaining ingredients except buns in a slow cooker; stir to blend. Add hamburgers; cover and cook on low setting for 3 to 4 hours. Serve on buns. Makes 6 sandwiches.

Steam Burgers

Roberta Oest, Astoria, IL

2 lbs. ground beef chuck
2-1/4 T. onion soup mix
1 T. Worcestershire sauce
1/4 t. pepper

1/2 c. water
8 to 10 hamburger buns,
  split
Optional: catsup

Brown beef in a skillet over medium heat; drain. Spoon beef into a slow cooker; stir in soup mix, sauce, pepper and water. Cover and cook on low setting for 2 to 4 hours, until heated through and liquid is absorbed. Spoon onto buns for sandwiches; top with catsup, if desired. Serves 8 to 10.

Pepper Steak

Pepper Steak

Ellen Sharp, Ashland, KY

1 lb. boneless beef round
  steak, cut into strips
2 green peppers, cut into
  strips
2 onions, sliced

2 14-1/2 oz. cans diced
  tomatoes
salt and pepper to taste

Combine all ingredients in a slow cooker. Cover and
cook on low setting for 6-1/2 to 7 hours. Serves 4.

Quick side

It's so easy to turn leftover roasts into the
best-tasting burritos. Warm tortillas by
heating them one at a time in a large skillet
over medium heat, flipping when they begin
to puff. Remove from heat and spread a
portion of warm beef on each tortilla; add
rice, sour cream, guacamole and pico de
gallo or salsa to taste. Roll up and serve!

Teriyaki Steak Subs

Virginia Watson, Scranton, PA

1/2 c. onion, chopped
1/2 c. soy sauce
1/4 c. red wine or beef broth
2 t. garlic, minced

1 T. fresh ginger, peeled and grated
1 T. sugar
3 lbs. beef round steak, cut crosswise
  into thirds

8 to 10 sub buns, split
Garnish: thinly sliced onion

In a bowl, combine all ingredients except beef, buns and garnish. Layer beef pieces in a slow cooker, spooning some of the onion mixture over each piece. Cover and cook on low setting for 6 to 7 hours, until beef is tender. Remove beef to a platter, reserving cooking liquid in slow cooker. Let beef stand several minutes before thinly slicing. To serve, place sliced beef on buns; top with sliced onion and some of the reserved cooking liquid. Makes 8 to 10 servings.

Teriyaki Steak Subs

Slow-Cooker Beef Taco Soup

Slow-Cooker Beef Taco Soup

Susan Ahlstrand, Post Falls, ID

1 lb. ground beef
1 onion, diced
1 clove garlic, minced
12-oz. bottle green taco sauce
4-oz. can green chiles

2 to 3 15-oz. cans black beans,
    drained and rinsed
15-1/4 oz. can corn, drained
15-oz. can tomato sauce
2 c. water

1-1/4 oz. pkg. taco seasoning mix
Garnish: sour cream, shredded
    Cheddar cheese, corn chips

Brown beef, onion and garlic in a large skillet over medium heat; drain. In a slow cooker, combine beef mixture and remaining ingredients except garnish. Cover and cook on high setting for one hour. Serve with sour cream, shredded cheese and corn chips. Serves 8 to 10.

Creamy Beef Stroganoff

Shelly Smith, Dana, IN

2 lbs. stew beef, cubed
salt and pepper to taste
2 10-3/4 oz. cans cream of
    mushroom soup

3 T. Worcestershire sauce
3-oz. pkg. cream cheese, cubed

16-oz. container sour cream
cooked rice or noodles

Place beef in a slow cooker; sprinkle with salt and pepper. Pour soup over top; add Worcestershire sauce. Cover and cook on low setting for 8 to 10 hours. Stir in cream cheese and sour cream 30 minutes before serving. Serve over rice or noodles. Serves 6 to 8.

Sally's Supreme Corned Beef

Sally Kohler, Webster, NY

2 to 3-lb. corned beef brisket
12-oz. bottle chili sauce

1.35-oz. pkg. onion soup mix
12-oz. can cola

cooked egg noodles

Place brisket in slow cooker. Mix remaining ingredients except noodles; pour over brisket. Cover and cook on low setting and cook for 6 to 8 hours. Slice beef and serve over noodles. Makes 4 to 6 servings.

Apple & Brown Sugar Corned Beef

Mary Lauff-Thompson, Doylestown, PA

3-lb. corned beef brisket
8 new redskin potatoes
4 carrots, peeled and
 chopped
1 onion, sliced

1 qt. apple juice
1 c. brown sugar, packed
1 T. Dijon or honey
 mustard

Place brisket in a slow cooker; add vegetables. In a bowl, combine juice, brown sugar and mustard; mix well. Drizzle juice mixture over brisket mixture; stir to coat evenly. Cover and cook on low setting for 8 to 10 hours, until brisket is very tender. Remove brisket from slow cooker; thinly slice. Serve sliced brisket with vegetables from slow cooker. Serves 6.

Roast Beef Hash

Carrie Bonikowske, Stevens Point, WI

1-1/2 to 2 lbs. stew beef,
 cubed
20-oz. pkg. refrigerated
 shredded hashbrowns

1 onion, chopped
1/4 c. butter, melted
1 c. beef broth
salt and pepper to taste

Combine all ingredients in a slow cooker. Cover and cook on low setting for 6 to 8 hours. Serves 4 to 6.

Chipotle Shredded Beef

Lisa Sett, Thousand Oaks, CA

2-1/2 lb. beef chuck roast,
 trimmed
14-oz. can diced tomatoes
7-oz. can chipotle sauce
4-oz. can diced green chiles
1 onion, chopped
2 T. chili powder
1 t. ground cumin

2 c. beef broth
salt and pepper to taste
6 to 8 6-inch corn
 tortillas, warmed
Garnish: shredded
 Cheddar cheese,
 shredded lettuce, sliced
 black olives, chopped
 tomato

Place roast in a slow cooker. Top with remaining ingredients except tortillas and garnish. Cover and cook on low setting for 8 to 10 hours. With 2 forks, shred roast in slow cooker; stir well. Spoon into warmed tortillas; add desired garnishes. Makes 6 to 8 servings.

Quick tip

Out of brown sugar? Whip some up by adding 1-1/2 teaspoons of molasses to one cup of white sugar. Mix well, and you've got sweet light brown sugar.

Chipotle Shredded Beef

Quick tip

Place onions in the freezer for
just 5 minutes before slicing them...
no more tears!

Tex-Mex Taco Joes

Tex-Mex Taco Joes

Sherry Cress, Salem, IN

3 lbs. ground beef, browned and drained
16-oz. can refried beans
10-oz. can enchilada sauce

1-1/4 oz. pkg. taco seasoning mix
16-oz. jar salsa
25 hot dog buns, split

Garnish: shredded Cheddar cheese, shredded lettuce, chopped tomatoes, sour cream

Place beef in a slow cooker. Stir in beans, enchilada sauce, seasoning mix and salsa. Cover and cook on low setting for 4 to 6 hours. To serve, fill each bun with 1/3 cup beef mixture; garnish as desired. Makes 25 sandwiches.

Slow-Cooker Sloppy Joes

Shelley Sparks, Amarillo, TX

1-1/2 lbs. ground beef
1 c. onion, chopped
2 cloves garlic, minced
3/4 c. catsup
1/2 c. green pepper, chopped

1/2 c. celery, chopped
1/4 c. water
1 T. brown sugar, packed
2 T. mustard
2 T. vinegar

2 T. Worcestershire sauce
1-1/2 t. chili powder
6 to 8 hamburger buns, toasted

In a skillet, brown beef, onion and garlic; drain and set aside. Combine remaining ingredients except buns in a slow cooker; stir in beef mixture. Cover; cook on low setting for 6 to 8 hours, or on high setting for 3 to 4 hours. Spoon onto buns. Serves 6 to 8.

Beef It Up

Easy-Peasy Bolognese Sauce

Mia Rossi, Charlotte, NC

1/4 lb. bacon, chopped
1 T. olive oil
1 onion, minced
3/4 c. celery, minced
2 carrots, peeled and minced
2 lbs. lean ground beef
salt and pepper to taste

1/4 c. white wine or chicken broth
2 28-oz. cans crushed tomatoes
3 bay leaves
1/4 c. fresh parsley, chopped
1/2 c. half-and-half

Cook bacon in a large skillet over medium heat until just crisp. Add oil, onion, celery and carrots; cook until vegetables are tender, about 5 minutes. Add beef; sprinkle with salt and pepper. Continue cooking until beef is almost completely browned, about 10 minutes; drain. Add wine or broth; cook for 3 to 4 minutes. Transfer beef mixture to a slow cooker; add tomatoes with juice and bay leaves. Cover and cook on low setting for 6 hours; season again with salt and pepper. Discard bay leaves; stir in half-and-half and parsley just before serving. Makes 10 to 12 servings.

Oh-So Easy Lasagna

April Longmore, Preston, ID

1 to 2 lbs. ground beef, browned and drained
26-oz. jar Parmesan & Romano pasta sauce
8-oz. pkg. bowtie pasta

12-oz. container cottage cheese
16-oz. pkg. shredded mozzarella cheese

Mix together ground beef and pasta sauce. In a slow cooker, layer half each of ground beef mixture, pasta, cottage cheese and shredded cheese. Repeat with remaining ingredients. Cover and cook on low setting for 6 to 8 hours, or on high setting for 3 to 4 hours. Serves 8.

Italian Meatball Subs

Clydia Mims, Effingham, SC

1 lb. ground beef
1 c. Italian-seasoned dry bread crumbs
1/2 c. grated Parmesan cheese
1 T. fresh parsley, minced

1 clove garlic, minced
1/2 c. milk
1 egg
1-1/2 t. salt
1/2 t. pepper
8 hot dog buns, split

Combine all ingredients except buns in a large bowl; mix well. Form into 2-inch balls and place in a slow cooker; pour Sauce over top. Cover and cook on low setting for 8 to 10 hours, or on high setting for 4 to 6 hours. To serve, place 3 to 4 meatballs on a bun; top with sauce from slow cooker. Makes 8 sandwiches.

Sauce:

28-oz. can tomato purée
28-oz. can Italian-style crushed tomatoes
1/2 c. grated Parmesan cheese

2 1-1/2 oz. pkgs. spaghetti sauce mix
salt and pepper to taste

Mix all ingredients in a saucepan; bring to a boil. Reduce heat and simmer until blended.

Italian Meatball Subs

Baja Steak

Baja Steak

Geneva Rogers, Gillette, WY.

1-1/2 lbs. boneless beef
  round steak, cut into
  serving-size pieces
2 c. frozen corn, thawed
  and drained
18-oz. jar chunky garden
  salsa
15-oz. can black beans,
  drained and rinsed

1 onion, chopped
1/2 c. water
1/2 t. salt
Optional: 1/8 t. red
  pepper flakes

Place beef in a slow cooker. Mix remaining ingredients together; pour over beef. Cover and cook on low setting for 8 to 9 hours. Serves 6.

Spanish Rice

Gloria Bills, Plymouth, MI

2 lbs. ground beef,
  browned and drained
2 onions, chopped
2 green peppers, chopped
28-oz. can diced
  tomatoes
8-oz. can tomato sauce

1 c. long-cooking rice,
  uncooked
1 c. water
2-1/2 t. chili powder
2-1/2 t. salt
2 t. Worcestershire sauce

Combine all ingredients in a slow cooker; stir thoroughly. Cover and cook on low setting for 6 to 8 hours, or on high setting for 3 to 4 hours. Serves 6.

Mexican Hamburgers

Ann Christie, Glasgow, KY

2 lbs. ground beef
2-1/4 c. water, divided
28-oz. can tomato purée
1 t. chili powder

pepper to taste
8 to 10 hamburger buns,
  split

Brown beef with one cup water in a skillet over medium heat; drain. Spoon beef into a slow cooker. Stir in remaining water and other ingredients except buns. Cover and cook on low setting for 4-1/2 to 5 hours, stirring occasionally, until heated through. Spoon beef mixture onto buns. Serves 8 to 10.

Quick tip

Long-cooking rice is best for slow-cooker recipes...it stays firm, while instant rice can overcook and become mushy.

Sweet & Savory Beef Sandwiches

Lisa Schneck, Lehighton, PA

12-oz. can beer or non-alcoholic beer
1 c. brown sugar, packed

24-oz. bottle catsup
3 to 4-lb. boneless beef roast
6 to 8 Kaiser rolls, split

Optional: banana pepper slices

Stir together beer, sugar and catsup in a slow cooker. Add roast and spoon mixture over top. Cover and cook on low setting for 7 to 8 hours. Remove roast and shred; return to juices in slow cooker. Serve shredded beef on rolls for sandwiches, topped with pepper slices if desired. Serves 6 to 8.

Slow-Cooker Swiss Steak

Cathy Callen, Lawton, OK

1-lb. beef round steak, cut into serving-size pieces

salt and pepper to taste
1.35-oz. pkg. onion soup mix

16-oz. can stewed tomatoes

Sprinkle steak with salt and pepper; place in a slow cooker. Add remaining ingredients. Cover and cook on low setting for 6 to 8 hours, or on high setting for 3 to 4 hours. Makes 4 servings.

Meatball Hoagies

Virginia Watson, Scranton, PA

1 lb. lean ground beef
1/2 c. Italian-flavored dry bread crumbs
1 egg, beaten

2 T. onion, minced
1 T. grated Parmesan cheese
1 t. salt
1 t. Worcestershire sauce

32-oz. jar pasta sauce
hoagie rolls, split
Garnish: sliced mozzarella cheese

In a large bowl, combine beef, bread crumbs, egg, onion, Parmesan cheese, salt and Worcestershire sauce. Using your hands, mix until just combined. Form into one-inch meatballs. Cook meatballs in a large skillet, turning occasionally, until browned on all sides. Remove meatballs to a slow cooker; top with pasta sauce. Cover and cook on low setting for about 2 hours, stirring after one hour. To serve, spoon several meatballs into each bun; top with a spoonful of sauce and a slice of cheese. Makes 6 to 8 servings.

Quick tip

Whip up your own Thousand Island dressing.
Just stir together 1/2 cup mayonnaise,
2 tablespoons catsup, one tablespoon
vinegar, 2 teaspoons sweet pickle relish and
sprinkle with salt and pepper to taste!

Sweet & Savory Beef Sandwiches

Homestyle Stuffed Peppers

Homestyle Stuffed Peppers

Carolyn Russell, Clyde, NC

1-1/2 lbs. ground beef
1 onion, finely chopped
1 c. instant rice, uncooked
4 green peppers, tops
  removed
15-oz. can tomato sauce
Optional: salt-free
  seasoning to taste

Mix together ground beef, onion and rice; spoon into peppers. Arrange peppers in a slow cooker; pour tomato sauce over top. Sprinkle with seasoning, if desired. Cover and cook on low setting for 5 to 6 hours. Serves 4.

Swedish Cabbage Rolls

Linda Sinclair, Valencia, CA

12 large leaves cabbage
1 egg, beaten
1/4 c. milk
1/4 c. onion, finely chopped
1 t. salt
1/4 t. pepper
1/2 lb. ground beef
1/2 lb. ground pork
1 c. cooked rice
8-oz. can tomato sauce
1 T. brown sugar, packed
1 T. lemon juice
1 t. Worcestershire sauce
Garnish: sour cream

Immerse cabbage leaves in a large kettle of boiling water for about 3 minutes, or until limp; drain well and set aside. Combine egg, milk, onion, salt, pepper, beef, pork and cooked rice; mix well. Place about 1/4 cup meat mixture in the center of each leaf; fold in sides and roll ends over meat. Arrange cabbage rolls in a slow cooker. Combine remaining ingredients and pour over rolls. Cover and cook on low setting for 7 to 9 hours. Spoon sauce over rolls and garnish with sour cream. Makes 6 servings.

Savory Tomato Brisket

Geneva Rogers, Gillette, WY

3 to 4-lb. beef brisket
28-oz. can Italian-style
  crushed tomatoes
1 red onion, chopped
2 T. red wine vinegar
2 T. Worcestershire sauce
1/2 t. smoke-flavored
  cooking sauce
4 cloves garlic, minced
1 T. brown sugar, packed
1 t. celery seed
1/2 t. salt
1 t. pepper
1/2 t. ground cumin
4 t. cornstarch
3 T. cold water

Place brisket in a slow cooker; set aside. In a large bowl, combine tomatoes with juice, onion, vinegar, sauces, garlic, brown sugar and seasonings. Pour tomato mixture over brisket. Cover and cook on low setting for 8 to 10 hours, until beef is very tender. Remove brisket to a serving plate; set aside and keep warm. In a saucepan over medium heat, combine water, cornstarch and 4 cups liquid from slow cooker. Bring to a boil; cook and stir for 2 minutes, or until mixture thickens. Serve brisket with gravy from saucepan. Serves 6 to 8.

Cajun Pot Roast

Kerry Mayer, Dunham Springs, LA

2-lb. boneless beef chuck roast
1 T. Cajun seasoning
1 onion, chopped
14-1/2 oz. can diced tomatoes with garlic
1/2 t. hot pepper sauce
1/8 t. pepper

Sprinkle roast with Cajun seasoning; rub to coat. Place roast in a slow cooker; top with onion. Combine remaining ingredients; pour over roast. Cover and cook on low setting for 8 to 10 hours. Serves 6.

Burgundy Meatloaf

Vickie

2 lbs. ground beef
2 eggs
1 c. soft bread crumbs
1 onion, chopped
1/2 c. Burgundy wine or beef broth
1/2 c. fresh parsley, chopped
1 T. fresh basil, chopped
1-1/2 t. salt
1/4 t. pepper
5 slices bacon
1 bay leaf
8-oz. can tomato sauce

Combine ground beef, eggs, crumbs, onion, wine or broth and seasonings in a large bowl; mix well and set aside. Criss-cross 3 bacon slices on a 12-inch square of aluminum foil. Form beef mixture into a 6-inch round loaf on top of bacon. Cut remaining bacon slices in half; arrange on top of meatloaf. Place bay leaf on top. Lift meatloaf by aluminum foil into a slow cooker; cover and cook on high setting for one hour. Reduce to low setting and continue cooking, covered, for an additional 4 hours. Remove meatloaf from slow cooker by lifting foil. Place on a serving platter, discarding foil, bacon and bay leaf. Warm tomato sauce and spoon over sliced meatloaf. Serves 4 to 6.

Magic Meatloaf

Beverly Tierney, Greenfield, IN

2 lbs. ground beef
1 egg, beaten
1/2 c. green pepper, chopped
1/2 c. onion, chopped
1 c. milk
1 c. saltine cracker crumbs
.87-oz. pkg. brown gravy mix
1-1/2 t. salt
6 to 8 new redskin potatoes

Mix all ingredients except potatoes in a large bowl. Mix well and form into a loaf; place in a lightly greased slow cooker. Arrange potatoes around meatloaf. Cover and cook on low setting for 8 to 10 hours, or on high setting for 3 to 5 hours. Serves 4 to 6.

Quick tip

Slow cookers are ideal for any country supper potluck. Tote them filled with your favorite spiced cider, stew, pulled pork or cobbler!

Magic Meatloaf

Teriyaki Beef

Teriyaki Beef

Molly Cool, Columbus, OH

1/3 c. teriyaki marinade
8-oz. can crushed
    pineapple
1-1/2 lb. boneless beef
    chuck steak

Spray a slow cooker with non-stick vegetable spray; add marinade and pineapple with juice. Place steak in marinade mixture. Cover and cook on high setting for 2-1/2 to 3-1/2 hours. Makes 4 servings.

Cattle Drive Stew

Karen Pilcher, Burleson, TX

1/2 lb. stew beef, cubed
16-oz. pkg. Kielbasa, sliced
1 onion, chopped
3 potatoes, peeled and
    chopped
28-oz. can baked beans

Arrange all ingredients in a slow cooker in the order shown. Cover and cook on high setting for 4 hours, or on low setting for 8 hours. Makes 6 to 8 servings.

Slow-Cooker Meatloaf

Marie Blackman, Crown Point, IN

1-1/2 lbs. ground beef
2 eggs
3/4 c. milk
1 onion, chopped
1 t. salt
1/4 t. pepper
3/4 c. bread crumbs
1/4 c. catsup
2 T. brown sugar, packed
1 t. dry mustard
1/4 t. nutmeg

Mix together beef, eggs, milk, onion, salt, pepper and bread crumbs; form mixture into a loaf and place in slow cooker. Cook on low 5 to 6 hours. Combine remaining ingredients; pour over top. Cook on high 15 additional minutes. Serves 4 to 6.

Quick tip

A garden-fresh side dish that's ready in a jiffy. Beat together one cup sour cream, 2 tablespoons vinegar and 4 tablespoons sugar. Fold in one peeled and thinly sliced cucumber; add salt and pepper to taste.

BBQ Cowboy Beans

Carrie Miller, Dry Fork, VA

1/2 lb. ground beef, browned and drained
6 to 8 slices bacon, crisply cooked and crumbled
15-oz. can lima beans
15-oz. can kidney beans
16-oz. can pork & beans
1/2 c. barbecue sauce
1/2 c. sugar
1/2 c. brown sugar, packed
1 t. smoke-flavored cooking sauce

Combine all ingredients in a slow cooker; stir thoroughly. Cover and cook on low setting for 3 to 4 hours. Makes 8 servings.

Coffee Roast Beef

Debra Oliver, Plainview, TX

3-lb. beef chuck roast
1.35-oz. pkg. onion soup mix
10-3/4 oz. can cream of mushroom soup
2 c. brewed coffee
2 t. cornstarch
2 t. water

Place roast in a slow cooker. Sprinkle with soup mix; spread soup on top and pour coffee over soup. Cover and cook on high setting for 6 to 8 hours, until roast is tender. Remove roast to a serving platter; cover to keep warm. In a cup, dissolve cornstarch in water; add to liquid in slow cooker. Cover and cook for 15 minutes, or until thickened. Serve roast with gravy. Serves 4 to 6.

Darn Good Cola-Chili Roast

Anna Rendell, Burnsville, MN

2-lb. beef chuck roast
1-oz. pkg. onion soup mix
12-oz. can cola
12-oz. bottle chili sauce
3 potatoes, peeled and cubed
3 carrots, peeled and sliced

Place roast in a slow cooker and sprinkle with soup mix. Pour cola and chili sauce over roast. Cover and cook on low setting for 6 hours. Add vegetables; cover and cook 2 more hours, or until roast and vegetables are tender. Makes 4 to 6 servings.

BBQ Cowboy Beans

California Chicken Tacos

California Chicken Tacos

Dawn Morgan, Glendora, CA

1 lb. boneless, skinless
   chicken breasts
1-1/4 oz. pkg. taco
   seasoning mix
16-oz. jar favorite salsa

8 to 10 corn taco shells
Garnish: shredded lettuce,
   diced tomatoes, sour
   cream, shredded
   Cheddar cheese

Combine all ingredients except taco shells and garnish.
Cover and cook on low setting for 6 to 8 hours, or on high
setting for 4 hours. Shred chicken and spoon into taco
shells; garnish as desired. Makes 8 to 10 tacos.

Carolina Chicken Pitas

Sharon Tillman, Hampton, VA

1 onion, chopped
1 lb. boneless, skinless
   chicken thighs
1 t. lemon-pepper
   seasoning

1/2 t. dried oregano
1/2 c. plain yogurt
4 pita bread rounds,
   halved and split

Combine all ingredients except yogurt and pitas in a slow
cooker; mix well. Cover and cook on low setting for 6 to
8 hours. Just before serving, remove chicken from slow
cooker and shred with 2 forks. Return shredded chicken
to slow cooker; stir in yogurt. Spoon into pita bread.
Makes 4 sandwiches.

Lemon-Garlic Chicken Tacos

Marion Sundberg, Ramona, CA

6 boneless, skinless
   chicken breasts
1 to 1-1/2 c. lemon juice or
   chicken broth
5 to 6 cloves garlic

salt and pepper to taste
12 corn taco shells
Garnish: shredded lettuce,
   chopped tomatoes,
   shredded Cheddar cheese

Place chicken in a slow cooker. Cover and cook on low
setting for 8 hours; drain. Shred chicken and return to
slow cooker; add lemon juice to cover, garlic, salt and
pepper. Cover and cook on low setting for an additional
4 to 5 hours. Serve in taco shells and garnish as desired.
Makes 12 tacos.

Quick tip

Use the last few minutes Lemon-Garlic
Chicken Tacos are cooking to whip up a
speedy black bean salad. Combine one cup
drained and rinsed black beans, 1/2 cup
frozen corn, 1/2 cup salsa and 1/4 teaspoon
cumin or chili powder; stir well.

Chicken Parmigiana

Diane Tracy, Lake Mary, FL

1 egg
3/4 c. milk
salt and pepper to taste
2 c. Italian-seasoned dry bread
 crumbs

4 boneless, skinless chicken
 breasts
2 T. oil
26-oz. jar spaghetti sauce, divided

1 to 2 c. shredded mozzarella
 cheese
cooked spaghetti

Beat together egg and milk in a deep bowl. Add salt and pepper; set aside. Place bread crumbs in a shallow bowl. Dip chicken breasts into egg mixture; coat with crumb mixture. Heat oil in a skillet over medium heat; cook chicken just until golden on both sides. Add one cup sauce to bottom of a slow cooker; top with chicken. Spoon remaining sauce over chicken. Cover and cook on low setting for 6 to 8 hours. About 15 minutes before serving, sprinkle cheese over top; cover until melted. Serve chicken and sauce over cooked spaghetti. Makes 4 servings.

Chicken Italiano

Tina Wright, Atlanta, GA

2 lbs. boneless, skinless chicken
 breasts, cut into strips
1/4 c. butter, melted
8-oz. container cream cheese with
 chives, softened

10-3/4 oz. can golden mushroom
 soup
.7-oz. pkg. Italian salad dressing
 mix

1/2 c. water
cooked bowtie pasta or rice

Place chicken in a slow cooker; set aside. In a medium bowl, combine melted butter, cream cheese, soup, dressing mix and water in a bowl; stir until blended and pour over chicken. Cover and cook on low setting for 6 to 8 hours. Stir well; serve over cooked pasta or rice. Serves 4 to 6.

Chicken Parmigiana

Quick tip

It's always best to fluff rice with a fork after cooking instead of stirring with a spoon...with a fork it's sure to be fluffy every time!

Rosemary & Thyme Chicken

Too-Easy Rotisserie Chicken

Sandra Sullivan, Aurora, CO

2 t. kosher salt
1 t. paprika
1 t. onion powder
1 t. Italian seasoning
1/2 t. dried thyme
1/2 t. cayenne pepper
1/2 t. pepper
1/8 t. chili powder
4 to 5-lb. roasting chicken
4 cloves garlic
1 onion, quartered

Combine spices in a bowl. Rub spice mixture over all sides of chicken. Place chicken, breast-side down, in a slow cooker. Put garlic and onion inside chicken cavity. Cover and cook on low setting for 8 to 10 hours, until juices run clear. Serves 4 to 6.

Honey-Glazed Chicken

Joshua Logan, Victoria, TX

8 pieces chicken
1/2 c. honey
1/4 c. butter, melted
2 T. soy sauce

Place chicken in a large plastic zipping bag. Drizzle with remaining ingredients; seal bag and squeeze to coat. Freeze. To prepare, thaw overnight in refrigerator. Add contents to a slow cooker. Cover and cook on low setting for about 8 hours, until chicken juices run clear. Makes 8 servings.

Rosemary & Thyme Chicken

Linda Sather, Corvallis, OR

3-lb. roasting chicken
1 to 2 T. garlic, minced
kosher salt to taste
1/2 onion, sliced into
  wedges
4 sprigs fresh rosemary
3 sprigs fresh thyme
seasoning salt to taste

Rub inside of chicken with garlic and kosher salt. Stuff with onion wedges and herb sprigs. Sprinkle seasoning salt on the outside of chicken; place in slow cooker. Cover and cook on low setting for 8 to 10 hours. Serves 4.

Chicken To Cheer For

Asian Chicken

Sarah Oravecz, Columbus, OH

3-1/2 lbs. boneless, skinless
  chicken breasts
1/3 c. creamy peanut butter

2 T. soy sauce
3 T. orange juice
1/8 t. pepper

cooked rice or noodles

Place chicken in a slow cooker. Combine remaining ingredients except rice or noodles in a slow cooker; spread over chicken. Cover and cook on low setting for 6 to 8 hours, until chicken is tender. Serve with cooked rice or noodles. Makes 6 to 8 servings

Thai Chicken & Rice

Carrie O'Shea, Marina Del Rey, CA

6 boneless, skinless chicken
  breasts or thighs, cut into strips
1 red pepper, sliced
1 onion, coarsely chopped
1/2 c. chicken broth
5 T. soy sauce, divided

3 cloves garlic, minced
1 T. ground cumin
1/2 t. red pepper flakes
salt and pepper to taste
2 T. cornstarch
2/3 c. creamy peanut butter

1/4 c. lime juice
cooked rice
Garnish: chopped fresh cilantro,
  chopped green onions, chopped
  peanuts

Arrange chicken, red pepper and onion in a slow cooker; set aside. In a bowl, combine broth and 4 tablespoons soy sauce; drizzle over chicken mixture. Add garlic and seasonings to slow cooker; stir to mix. Cover and cook on low setting for 4-1/2 to 5 hours, until chicken is no longer pink in the center. Remove one cup liquid from slow cooker; mix with cornstarch, peanut butter, lime juice and remaining soy sauce in a bowl. Stir mixture back into slow cooker; increase heat to high setting. Cover and cook for 30 minutes. Spoon over rice to serve; garnish as desired. Serves 6.

Ruby Chicken

Ellie Brandel, Milwaukie, OR

2 lbs. boneless, skinless chicken
  breasts, cubed
1 onion, chopped
12-oz. can frozen orange juice
  concentrate, thawed

zest of 1 orange
1 orange, chopped
12-oz. pkg. fresh cranberries
1 c. sugar
2 T. oil

2 t. salt
1 t. pumpkin pie spice
cooked rice

Add all ingredients except rice to a slow cooker. Cover and cook on low setting for 6 to 8 hours, until chicken juices run clear. Serve chicken and sauce from slow cooker over cooked rice. Makes 8 servings.

Thai Chicken & Rice

Quick tip

Come on, try chopsticks when serving Asian Chicken! Don't forget to pick up some fortune cookies too...sure to make for a fun-filled dinner.

Quick tip

If there seems to be a bit too much liquid inside the slow cooker, and it's almost dinnertime, tilt the lid and turn the slow cooker to its high setting...soon the liquid will begin to evaporate.

Maple Praline Chicken

Maple Praline Chicken

Jill Valentine, Jackson, TN

6 boneless, skinless chicken
  breasts
2 T. Cajun seasoning

1/4 c. butter, melted
1/2 c. maple syrup
2 T. brown sugar, packed

1 c. chopped pecans
6-oz. pkg. long-grain and wild
rice, cooked

Sprinkle chicken with Cajun seasoning. In a skillet over medium-high heat, cook chicken in butter until golden. Arrange chicken in a slow cooker. In a bowl, mix together syrup, brown sugar and pecans; spoon over chicken. Cover and cook on low setting for 6 to 8 hours. Serve with cooked rice. Serves 6.

Just Peachy Chicken

Elizabeth Blackstone, Racine, WI

4 boneless, skinless chicken thighs
2 sweet potatoes, peeled and
  cubed

1 onion, chopped
2 T. cold water
3 T. cornstarch

1/2 c. peach preserves

Place chicken in a slow cooker; add sweet potatoes and onion. Cover and cook on low setting for 7 to 8 hours. Pour off juices from slow cooker into a saucepan; set aside. Cover chicken, sweet potatoes and onion to keep warm. In a heavy saucepan, combine water and cornstarch; mix well. Add reserved juices from slow cooker; stir in preserves. Cook and stir over medium heat, stirring frequently, until mixture boils and thickens. Cook for 2 minutes; pour over chicken and vegetables. Serves 4.

Honey Chicken Wings

Karen Mooney, Newnan, GA

3 lbs. chicken wings
salt and pepper
2 c. honey

1 c. soy sauce
1/2 c. catsup
1/4 c. oil

2 cloves garlic, minced

Sprinkle wings with salt and pepper. Arrange on a broiler pan; broil 4 to 5 inches from heat until golden, about 10 minutes per side. Transfer wings to a slow cooker and set aside. Combine remaining ingredients in a small bowl; pour over wings. Cover and cook on low setting for 4 to 5 hours, or on high setting for 2 to 2-1/2 hours. Makes about 2-1/2 dozen.

Chicken To Cheer For

Chicken Stew Over Biscuits

Debi Piper, Vicksburg, MI

2 c. water

3/4 c. white wine or chicken broth

2 .87-oz. pkgs. chicken gravy mix

2 cloves garlic, minced

1 T. fresh parsley, minced

1 to 2 t. chicken bouillon granules

1/2 t. pepper

1 onion, cut into 8 wedges

5 carrots, peeled and cut into 1-inch pieces

4 skinless, boneless chicken breasts, cut into bite-size pieces

3 T. all-purpose flour

1/3 c. cold water

16.3-oz. tube refrigerated large buttermilk biscuits, baked

Combine first 7 ingredients in a slow cooker; mix until blended. Add onion, carrots and chicken; cover and cook on low setting for 7 to 8 hours. In a small bowl, stir together flour and cold water until smooth; gradually stir into slow cooker. Increase setting to high; cover and cook for one hour. Place biscuits in soup bowls; top with stew. Makes 4 to 6 servings.

Southern Chicken & Dumplings

Stephanie Lucius, Powder Springs, GA

3 10-3/4 oz. cans cream of chicken soup

1/4 c. onion, diced

6 boneless, skinless chicken breasts

3-3/4 c. water

3 12-oz. tubes refrigerated biscuits, quartered

Pour soup into a slow cooker; add onion and chicken. Pour in enough water to cover chicken. Cover and cook on low setting for 6 to 8 hours, or on high setting for 4 to 6 hours. About 45 minutes before serving, turn slow cooker to high setting. Remove chicken with a slotted spoon; shred into bite-size pieces and return to slow cooker. Drop biscuit quarters into slow cooker; stir well. Replace lid and cook for 35 minutes more, or until dumplings are done. Stir and serve. Serves 6 to 8.

Chicken with Mushroom Gravy

Jo White, Philadelphia, TN

3 boneless, skinless chicken breasts, halved

salt and pepper to taste

1/4 c. chicken broth

10-3/4 oz. can cream of chicken soup

4-oz. can sliced mushrooms, drained

Place chicken in a slow cooker; sprinkle with salt and pepper. Mix together broth and soup; pour over chicken. Stir in mushrooms. Cover and cook on low setting for 7 to 9 hours, or on high setting for 3 to 4 hours. Serves 4.

Southern Chicken & Dumplings

Mexican Chicken

Nacho Chicken & Rice

Candace Whitelock, Seaford, DE

1 lb. boneless, skinless
chicken breasts, cubed
2 10-3/4 oz. cans Cheddar
cheese soup
1-1/4 c. water
16-oz. jar chunky salsa
1-1/4 c. long-cooking rice,
uncooked

Combine all ingredients in a slow cooker. Cover and cook on low setting for about 5 hours, or until chicken and rice are tender. Serves 6 to 8.

Mexican Chicken

Stephanie Smith, Mansfield, TX

15-oz. can black beans,
drained and rinsed
2 15-1/4 oz. cans corn,
drained
1 c. picante sauce, divided
2 lbs. boneless, skinless
chicken breasts
Garnish: shredded
Cheddar cheese
12 8-inch flour tortillas

Mix together beans, corn and 1/2 cup picante sauce in a slow cooker. Place chicken on top; pour remaining picante sauce over chicken. Cover and cook on high setting for 2-1/2 hours, or until chicken is tender. Shred chicken and return to slow cooker. Sprinkle with cheese; cover and cook until melted. Serve with tortillas. Serves 6.

Tex-Mex Chicken

Carla Hutto, Garrison, TX

5 to 6 boneless, skinless
chicken breasts
10-3/4 oz. can cream of
mushroom soup
10-3/4 oz. can cream of
chicken soup
10-oz. can diced tomatoes
with green chiles
corn chips
Garnish: shredded
Cheddar cheese

Place chicken in a slow cooker. Stir together soups and tomatoes; pour over chicken. Cover and cook on low setting for 8 to 10 hours. Spoon over corn chips; sprinkle with shredded cheese. Serves 4 to 6.

Quick tip

Try sprinkling chicken with a bit of fajita seasoning while cooking. What a flavor boost!

BBQ Chicken Sandwiches

Tina Dammrich, St. Louis, MO

4-lb. chicken

1-1/2 to 2 c. hickory smoke-flavored barbecue sauce

8 to 10 sandwich buns, split

Place chicken in a stockpot. Add water to cover and simmer until tender, about one hour. Remove chicken and cool; pull meat from bones. Place chicken in a slow cooker; cover with barbecue sauce. Cover and cook on high setting for 3 to 5 hours, stirring every 30 minutes. Chicken will shred during stirring. Serve on buns. Makes 8 to 10 sandwiches.

Sloppy Joe Chicken

Kathi Downey, Lompoc, CA

6 skinless chicken thighs

8-oz. can tomato sauce

1-1/2 oz. pkg. Sloppy Joe mix

2 T. honey

cooked rice

Place chicken in a slow cooker. Combine remaining ingredients except rice; pour over chicken. Cover and cook on low setting for 6 hours. Discard bones. Serve chicken and sauce over cooked rice. Serves 4.

Chicken-Stuffing Sandwiches

Amber Beckman, Garden City, MI

50-oz. can chicken

6-oz. pkg. chicken-flavored stuffing mix

10-3/4 oz. can cream of chicken soup

10-1/2 oz. can chicken broth

20 to 25 sandwich buns, split

Combine chicken with juice and remaining ingredients except buns in a slow cooker. Cover and cook on low setting for 4 hours, or on high setting for 2 hours. Spoon onto sandwich buns. Makes 20 to 25 sandwiches.

Quick tip

Keep salad tossing simple...add ingredients to a plastic zipping bag, seal, then shake!

Sloppy Joe Chicken

Tomato & Artichoke Chicken

Sweet & Spicy Chicken

Annette Ingram, Grand Rapids, MI

4 to 6 boneless, skinless
  chicken breasts
salt and pepper to taste

12-oz. jar orange marmalade
1/2 c. chicken broth
1-1/2 t. curry powder

1/2 t. cayenne pepper
Optional: 1/8 t. ground ginger

Sprinkle chicken with salt and pepper; place in a slow cooker. In a bowl, whisk together marmalade, broth and spices. Pour over chicken. Cover and cook on low setting for 5 to 7 hours, or on high setting for 3 to 4 hours, turning chicken halfway through cooking. Serves 4 to 6.

Tomato & Artichoke Chicken

Rachel Boyd, Defiance, OH

4 boneless, skinless chicken
  breasts
3 T. Italian salad dressing
1 t. Italian seasoning
1/2 onion, very thinly sliced

4 cloves garlic, minced
14-1/2 oz. can diced tomatoes,
  drained
14-oz. can quartered artichoke
  hearts, drained

2 to 3 T. dried parsley
cooked spaghetti

Place chicken in a slow cooker. Combine remaining ingredients and spoon over chicken. Cover and cook on low setting for 4 to 5 hours, until chicken juices run clear. To serve, spoon chicken mixture over cooked spaghetti. Serves 4 to 6.

Caribbean Chicken & Veggies

Amy Bradsher, Roxboro, NC

1 lb. boneless, skinless chicken
  tenders
1 c. canned diced pineapple with
  juice

1 onion, coarsely chopped
1 green pepper, coarsely chopped
3/4 c. Caribbean-style marinade
2 c. canned black beans, drained

1 lb. broccoli, cut into bite-size
  flowerets
cooked rice

Combine chicken, pineapple with juice, onion, green pepper and marinade in a slow cooker. Cover and cook on low setting for 4 to 5 hours, until chicken is nearly cooked. Add black beans and broccoli. Cover and cook for another hour, or until broccoli is tender. Serve chicken mixture over cooked rice. Makes 4 to 6 servings.

Chicken To Cheer For

Mozzarella Chicken & Rice

Jennifer Martineau, Delaware, OH

8 boneless, skinless
  chicken breasts
1/4 t. salt
1/8 t. pepper
1 onion, chopped
2 green peppers, coarsely
  chopped
2 c. pasta sauce
1 c. shredded mozzarella
  cheese
cooked orzo pasta or rice

Place chicken in a slow cooker; sprinkle with salt and pepper. Top with onion and green peppers; pour pasta sauce over top. Cover and cook on low setting for 4 to 5 hours. Stir well and sprinkle with cheese. Let stand for 5 minutes, until cheese is melted. Serve over cooked pasta or rice. Serves 8.

Orange-Glazed Chicken

Anna McMaster, Portland, OR

6 boneless, skinless
  chicken breasts
6-oz. can frozen orange
  juice concentrate,
  partially thawed
1 onion, diced
1 clove garlic, minced
1/2 t. dried rosemary
salt and pepper to taste
1/4 c. cold water
2 T. cornstarch

Place chicken in a slow cooker. Combine remaining ingredients except for water and cornstarch and spoon over chicken. Cover and cook on low setting for 7 to 9 hours. Remove chicken from slow cooker; keep warm. In a bowl, mix together water and cornstarch; drizzle into juices in slow cooker. Partially cover slow cooker; cook on high setting until sauce is thick and bubbly, about 15 to 30 minutes. Serve sauce with sliced chicken. Serves 6.

Aloha Chicken

Yvonne Van Brimmer, Apple Valley, CA

4 lbs. boneless, skinless
  chicken
20-oz. can pineapple
  chunks
11-oz. can mandarin
  oranges, drained
1 green or red pepper,
  chopped
1/4 c. onion, chopped
1 clove garlic, minced
1 T. soy sauce
1 t. fresh ginger, peeled
  and grated

Arrange chicken in a slow cooker; set aside. Combine remaining ingredients; pour over chicken. Cover and cook on low setting for 8 to 10 hours. Serves 8 to 10.

Quick tip

Resist the urge to lift the lid of your slow cooker to take a peek! Lifting the lid lets out the heat and makes cooking time longer.

Orange-Glazed Chicken

Quick side

Try a new side dish tonight...barley pilaf. Simply prepare quick-cooking barley with chicken broth instead of water, seasoning it with a little chopped onion and parsley. Filling, quick and tasty!

Barbecued Beer Chicken

Bacon-Swiss BBQ Chicken

Michelle Crabtree, Lee's Summit, MO

6 boneless, skinless chicken
  breasts
26-oz. bottle barbecue sauce

6 slices bacon, halved and crisply
  cooked
6 slices Swiss cheese

Place chicken in a slow cooker; cover with barbecue sauce. Cover and cook on low setting for 8 to 9 hours. Arrange 2 strips halved bacon over each piece of chicken; top with cheese slices. Cover and cook on high setting until cheese melts, about 15 minutes. Makes 6 servings.

Barbecued Beer Chicken

Kristy Markners, Fort Mill, SC

3 to 4-lb. roasting chicken
1/4 c. barbecue seasoning

12-oz. bottle regular or
  non-alcoholic beer

Spray a large slow cooker with non-stick vegetable spray. Carefully loosen skin from chicken. Rub seasoning generously under and on top of skin. Place chicken in a slow cooker; pour beer over chicken. Cover and cook on low setting for 8 hours. Serves 6.

Pulled BBQ Chicken

Jenita Davison, La Plata, MO

6 boneless, skinless chicken
  breasts
18-oz. bottle sweet onion barbecue
  sauce, or other favorite sauce

1/2 c. Italian salad dressing
1/4 c. light brown sugar, packed
2 T. Worcestershire sauce
sandwich buns, split

Place chicken in a slow cooker. Combine remaining ingredients except buns; spoon over chicken. Cover and cook on low setting for 6 to 8 hours, or on high setting for 3 to 4 hours. Using 2 forks, shred chicken in the sauce; stir. Serve chicken mixture spooned onto buns. Makes 6 servings.

Chicken Gravy for a Crowd

Bekah Brooks, Bluffton, IN

3 26-oz. cans cream of mushroom
  soup
16-oz. container sour cream
6 boneless, skinless chicken
  breasts

4 c. cooked brown rice
3 c. frozen corn, thawed
1 T. onion, minced
1 T. dried parsley
1 t. salt

1/2 t. pepper
mashed potatoes, toasted bread or
  split biscuits

In a large bowl, stir together soup and sour cream. Spread a one-inch layer of soup mixture in the bottom of a large slow cooker. Arrange chicken on top; spoon remaining soup mixture over chicken. Cover and cook on low setting for 6 to 8 hours, until chicken is very tender. Cut up chicken into bite-size pieces; return to slow cooker. Add remaining ingredients except potatoes, toast or biscuits; stir well. Cover and cook for another 30 minutes, or until heated through. To serve, ladle chicken and gravy over mashed potatoes, slices of toast or split biscuits. Serves 15 to 20.

Creamy Chicken & Noodles

Melissa Dennis, Marysville, OH

3 to 4 boneless, skinless chicken
  breasts
1/2 c. butter, sliced

2 10-3/4 oz. cans cream of chicken
  soup
4 10-1/2 oz. cans chicken broth

24-oz. pkg. frozen egg noodles

Combine all ingredients except noodles in a slow cooker. Cover and cook on low setting for 8 hours. One hour before serving, remove chicken, shred and return to slow cooker. Stir in frozen noodles; cover and cook on low setting for one hour. Serve in soup bowls. Serves 4 to 6.

Quick tip

Fill a basket with the fixin's for a simple supper like Creamy Chicken & Noodles and deliver to new parents...how thoughtful!

Creamy Chicken & Noodles

Greek Chicken Pitas

Quick tip

Rolls and buns will drip less when filled with juicy slow-cooked meat if they're toasted first.

Creamy Chicken Sandwiches

Darcie Meligan, Mansfield, OH

2 13-oz. cans chicken, drained
10-3/4 oz. can cream of chicken
  soup

10-3/4 oz. can cream of mushroom
  soup
1 t. garlic powder

pepper to taste
1 c. potato chips, coarsely crushed
8 to 10 buns, split

Mix together chicken and soups; add seasonings and crushed chips. Spoon into a slow cooker; cover and cook on high setting for 4 hours. Serve on buns. Makes 8 to 10 sandwiches.

Greek Chicken Pitas

Peggy Pelfrey, Ashland City, TN

1 onion, diced
3 cloves garlic, minced
1 lb. boneless, skinless chicken
  breasts, cut into strips

1 t. lemon-pepper seasoning
1/2 t. dried oregano
1/4 t. allspice
1/4 c. plain yogurt

1/4 c. sour cream
1/2 c. cucumber, peeled and diced
4 rounds pita bread, halved and
  split

Place onion and garlic in a slow cooker; set aside. Sprinkle chicken with seasonings; add to slow cooker. Cover and cook on high setting for 6 hours. Meanwhile, stir together yogurt, sour cream and cucumber in a small bowl; chill. Fill pita halves with chicken mixture and drizzle with yogurt sauce. Makes 4 sandwiches.

"Rotisserie" Chicken

Ann Mathis, Biscoe, AR

3 to 4-lb. broiler chicken
2 T. paprika
2 T. garlic powder, or 3 cloves
  garlic, minced

1-1/2 t. onion powder
1 t. salt
1/2 t. pepper

Optional: 1/2 t. cayenne pepper
3 to 4 t. water

Spray a slow cooker with non-stick vegetable spray. Add chicken breast-side up. In a small bowl, combine remaining ingredients except water; stir in water by teaspoonfuls until a paste forms. Coat chicken inside and out with paste. Cover and cook on low setting for 6 to 7 hours, or on high setting for 3-1/2 to 4-1/2 hours, until a meat thermometer inserted in thickest part of the thigh registers 180 degrees. Remove to a platter; let stand several minutes before slicing. Makes 6 servings.

Fiesta Chicken Pronto

Kristi Duis, Maple Plain, MN

8 boneless, skinless
 chicken breasts
16-oz. can black beans,
 drained and rinsed
10-3/4 oz. can cream
 of chicken soup
2 T. taco seasoning mix
1/4 c. salsa

Arrange chicken in a slow cooker. Combine remaining ingredients and pour over chicken. Cover and cook on high setting for 3 hours. Serves 8.

Cilantro-Lime Chicken

Sally Kelly, Akron, OH

3 boneless, skinless
 chicken breasts
2 14-1/2 oz. cans petite
 diced tomatoes with
 green chiles
2 T. lime juice
1/4 c. fresh cilantro,
 chopped
1-1/4 oz. pkg. taco
 seasoning mix
cooked rice

Combine all ingredients except rice in a slow cooker. Cover and cook on low setting for about 6 hours, until chicken is no longer pink in the center. Remove chicken from slow cooker; shred and return to juices in slow cooker. Serve chicken and juices from slow cooker over rice. Serves 3 to 4.

Make-Ahead Chipotle Burritos

Lorrie Coop, Munday, TX

2 lbs. boneless, skinless
 chicken breasts
2 15-1/2 oz. cans black
 beans, drained and
 rinsed
2 11-oz. cans corn, drained
20-oz. jar salsa
1 canned chipotle pepper
 in adobo sauce, chopped
2 t. chili powder
2 t. ground cumin
2 t. dried oregano
1 T. salt
flour or corn tortillas
Garnish: sour cream,
 sliced avocado, shredded
 Cheddar cheese

Divide chicken between 2 one-gallon plastic zipping freezer bags; set aside. In a large bowl, combine all ingredients except tortillas and garnish; divide between bags. Seal and flatten bags; freeze. To prepare, thaw one bag in refrigerator for 24 hours; place contents of bag in a slow cooker. Cover and cook on low setting for 8 hours, until chicken is very tender. Remove chicken and shred using 2 forks. Return chicken to slow cooker; stir to mix. Serve chicken mixture on tortillas, garnished as desired. Serves 6.

Make-Ahead Chipotle Burritos

Fantastic 40-Clove Chicken

Debbie's Cheesy Chicken

Debbie Anderson, Lafayette, IN

6 boneless, skinless
  chicken breasts
garlic powder to taste
salt and pepper to taste
2 10-3/4 oz. cans cream
  of chicken soup

10-3/4 oz. can Cheddar
  cheese soup
cooked rice or noodles

Place chicken in a slow cooker; sprinkle with garlic powder, salt and pepper. Mix together soups and pour over chicken. Cover and cook on low setting for 6 to 8 hours. Serve over rice or noodles. Serves 6.

Charlene's Ritzy Chicken

Dottie Croyle, Perry, OH

10-3/4 oz. can cream of
  chicken soup
1 pt. sour cream
1 sleeve round buttery
  crackers, crushed

1/2 c. butter, melted
4 to 6 boneless, skinless
  chicken breasts
mashed potatoes

Combine soup and sour cream in a small bowl; set aside. In a separate bowl, mix together crackers and butter. Place chicken in a slow cooker; spoon soup mixture over top and sprinkle with cracker mixture. Cover and cook on low setting for 7 to 9 hours, or on high setting for 4 to 5 hours. Serve over mashed potatoes. Serves 4 to 6.

Fantastic 40-Clove Chicken

Amy James, Fayetteville, AR

4 boneless, skinless
  chicken breasts
2 t. salt
1 t. pepper
40 cloves garlic, peeled
3/4 c. dry white wine or
  chicken broth

1 t. dried thyme
1-1/2 t. dried rosemary
1 bay leaf
1 T. butter

Season chicken with salt and pepper; place in a slow cooker. Add garlic, wine or broth and seasonings to slow cooker. Cover and cook on low setting for 4 to 6 hours, until chicken juices run clear. Remove chicken from slow cooker and pour juices through a strainer, mashing some garlic cloves through as well. Discard bay leaf. Cook juice mixture in a saucepan over high heat until thickened, about 6 to 8 minutes. Add butter to sauce; stir until mixed. Drizzle sauce over chicken. Serves 6 to 8.

Quick tip

Crunchy veggies make a nice go-with at dinnertime...just for fun, serve veggie dip in a hollowed-out round loaf of bread.

Chicken Cacciatore

Mary Whitacre, Mount Vernon, OH

1 lb. boneless, skinless
chicken breasts
26-oz. jar chunky garden
vegetable spaghetti
sauce
1 zucchini, chopped
1 green pepper, chopped
1 sweet onion, chopped
cooked wide egg noodles
or spaghetti
Garnish: chopped black
olives, shredded
Parmesan cheese

Place chicken in a slow cooker; pour sauce over top.
Add vegetables. Cover and cook on low setting for 6 to
8 hours. Spoon over wide noodles or spaghetti. Garnish
with black olives and Parmesan cheese. Serves 4.

Lemony "Baked" Chicken

Sharon Lundberg, Longwood, FL

3 to 4-lb. roasting chicken
2 T. olive oil
1 lemon
2 cloves garlic, minced
1 t. dried parsley
salt and pepper to taste

Pat chicken dry with a paper towel; rub with oil. Put
whole lemon inside chicken; place in slow cooker.
Sprinkle with garlic, parsley, salt and pepper. Cover and
cook on high setting for one hour. Turn to low setting
and cook an additional 6 to 7 hours. Makes 4 servings.

Chicken with Artichokes & Capers

Sandra Sullivan, Aurora, CT

3 lbs. boneless, skinless
chicken thighs
salt and pepper to taste
14-1/2 oz. can diced
tomatoes
14-oz. can artichoke
hearts, drained
1/4 c. capers
2 to 3 cloves garlic,
thinly sliced
8-oz. pkg. sliced
mushrooms
3 tomatoes, chopped
16-oz. pkg. spaghetti,
cooked

Season chicken with salt and pepper; place in a slow
cooker. Spoon canned tomatoes with juice, artichokes,
capers and garlic over chicken. Cover and cook on high
setting for 3 to 4 hours, until chicken juices run clear.
Stir in fresh tomatoes and mushrooms during the last
30 minutes of cooking. Serve chicken and sauce over
spaghetti. Serves 6 to 8.

Quick tip

When making a garden-fresh recipe like
Chicken Cacciatore, use a mixture of veggies
from the garden...just as tasty with any
favorite combinations!

Chicken wih Artichokes & Capers

Joan's Chicken Stuffing Casserole

Joan's Chicken Stuffing Casserole

Joan Brochu, Harwich, MA

12-oz. pkg. chicken stuffing mix
3 10-3/4 oz. cans cream of chicken
  soup, divided

1/2 c. milk
3 to 4 c. cooked chicken, cubed

12-oz. pkg. shredded Cheddar
  cheese

Prepare stuffing mix according to package directions; place in a slow cooker. Stir in 2 cans soup. In a separate bowl, stir together remaining soup, milk and chicken. Add to slow cooker. Spread cheese over top. Cover and cook on low setting for 4 to 6 hours, or on high setting for 2 to 3 hours. Serves 6.

Creamy Herbed Chicken

Cathy Neeley, North Logan, UT

4 boneless, skinless chicken
  breasts
10-3/4 oz. can cream of chicken
  with herbs soup

10-3/4 oz. can cream of mushroom
  with roasted garlic soup
1.2-oz. pkg. savory garlic & herb
  soup mix

2/3 c. water
cooked rice or noodles

Place chicken in a slow cooker. Combine soups, soup mix and water; pour over top. Cover and cook chicken on low setting for 6 to 8 hours, or on high setting for 3 to 4 hours. Serve over rice or noodles. Serves 4.

Creamy Chicken & Veggies

Shirley Howie, Foxboro, MA

1 onion, diced
6 new redskin potatoes, quartered
2 c. carrots, peeled and sliced
1 c. sliced mushrooms
2 lbs. boneless, skinless chicken
  thighs

10-3/4 oz. can cream of mushroom
  soup
2/3 c. chicken broth
1/4 c. all-purpose flour

1-oz. pkg. onion soup mix
1/2 t. poultry seasoning
1/2 t. dried thyme

Combine vegetables in a 5-quart slow cooker; arrange chicken thighs over vegetables. Stir together remaining ingredients in a bowl; spoon over chicken. Cover and cook on low setting for 4 to 5 hours, until chicken juices run clear when pierced. Makes 4 to 6 servings.

Chicken To Cheer For

Jason's Chicken Burritos

Jason Nicholson, Westerville, OH

6 boneless, skinless
  chicken breasts
15-1/4 oz. can corn,
  drained
16-oz. can black beans,
  drained and rinsed

16-oz. jar salsa
6 to 8 10-inch flour tortillas
Garnish: shredded
  Cheddar cheese, sour
  cream, salsa

Combine chicken, corn, beans and salsa in a slow cooker.
Cover and cook on low setting for 8 to 10 hours, or on
high setting for 4 to 6 hours. Shred chicken; stir back
into slow cooker. Roll up in tortillas; garnish as desired.
Makes 6 to 8 servings.

Slow-Cooker Chicken Fajitas

Karen Campbell, Canton, IL

3 green, yellow or red
  peppers, sliced
2 onions, sliced
2 T. garlic, finely minced
8 boneless, skinless
  chicken breasts, cut into
  thin strips
2 1-1/4 oz. pkgs. taco
  seasoning mix

1 t. coarse salt, divided
1/2 c. olive oil
8 to 12 flour tortillas
Garnish: salsa,
  guacamole, sour cream,
  shredded Colby Jack
  cheese, chopped black
  olives, diced tomatoes,
  shredded lettuce

Layer half each of peppers, onions, garlic and chicken in
a slow cooker; sprinkle with one package taco seasoning
and 1/2 teaspoon salt. Repeat layering; drizzle with oil.
Cover and cook on low setting for 4 to 6 hours, until
chicken is fully cooked and juices run clear. Stir to
combine. To serve, spoon chicken mixture onto tortillas,
adding desired toppings. Serves 4 to 6.

Chicken Mexi-Wraps

Marie Cordalis, Spokane, WA

3 boneless, skinless
  chicken breasts
1/2 c. salsa
8 10-inch flour tortillas,
  warmed

1 c. shredded Cheddar or
  Monterey Jack cheese
Garnish: shredded lettuce,
  chopped tomatoes, sour
  cream

Place chicken in a slow cooker; top with salsa. Cover
and cook on low setting for 6 to 8 hours. Remove chicken
from slow cooker; shred with a fork. Stir into juices in
slow cooker. Spoon chicken into warmed tortillas; top
with cheese and garnish as desired. Roll up. Makes
8 servings.

Quick tip

Save those cilantro stems! They have a
slightly sweet, herbal flavor that goes really
well in salads or any other recipe that calls
for cilantro.

Chicken Mexi-Wraps

🍴 *Quick side*

A quick go-with for a slow-cooker meal... toss steamed green beans, broccoli or zucchini with a little olive oil and chopped fresh herbs.

Winter Barbecued Chicken

Winter Barbecued Chicken

Mia Rossi, Charlotte, NC

1-1/2 t. paprika	3 lbs. chicken	2 T. cider vinegar
1/2 t. garlic powder	1/2 c. cola	Optional: 2 T. bourbon
2 t. salt	1/3 c. catsup	1 lemon, sliced
1/2 t. pepper	1/4 c. light brown sugar, packed	

In a bowl, stir together seasonings. Place chicken pieces in a slow cooker and sprinkle with seasoning mixture; toss to coat. In a separate bowl, whisk together remaining ingredients except lemon. Pour cola mixture over chicken; place lemon slices on top. Cover and cook on low setting for 6 to 7 hours, until chicken juices run clear. Remove chicken to a serving platter and discard lemon. Spoon sauce in slow cooker over chicken. Serves 6 to 8.

Autumn Nutmeg Chicken

Marilyn Morel, Keene, NH

6 boneless, skinless chicken breast halves	2 10-3/4 oz. cans cream of mushroom soup	1/4 t. dried rosemary
1 to 2 T. oil	1/2 c. sour cream	1/4 t. dried sage
1 onion, chopped	1/2 c. milk	1/4 t. dried thyme
1/4 c. fresh parsley, minced	1 T. nutmeg	cooked rice

In a skillet over medium heat, brown chicken in oil; reserve drippings. Arrange chicken in a slow cooker; set aside. Sauté onion and parsley in reserved drippings until onion is tender. Add remaining ingredients except rice; mix well and pour over chicken. Cover and cook on low setting for 5 hours, or until juices run clear when chicken is pierced. Serve over cooked rice. Makes 6 servings.

Chicken To Cheer For

Chicken Cordon Bleu

Debi Gilpin, Uniontown, PA

4 to 6 boneless, skinless
  chicken breasts
4 to 6 thin slices cooked
  ham

4 to 6 slices Swiss cheese
10-3/4 oz. can cream of
  mushroom soup
1/4 c. milk

Place each chicken breast in a plastic zipping bag; pound to flatten. Top each with a slice of ham and a slice of cheese; roll up and secure with a toothpick. Arrange rolls in a slow cooker in layers. Mix soup and milk; pour over chicken. Cover and cook on low setting for 4 to 6 hours, until chicken is no longer pink inside. To serve, remove toothpicks and arrange chicken rolls on serving plate; spoon sauce from slow cooker over rolls. Makes 4 to 6 servings.

Orange-Glazed Cornish Hens

Jo Ann

2 20-oz. Cornish game
  hens
salt and pepper to taste
8-oz. pkg. chicken-flavored
  stuffing mix, prepared
1 c. chicken broth
1 orange, sliced

1/4 c. orange juice
1/4 t. orange zest
2 T. honey
1 T. lemon juice
1-1/2 t. oil

Sprinkle hens inside and out with salt and pepper. Spoon prepared stuffing loosely into hens and truss closed. Place hens, neck-end down, in a large slow cooker. Stir together remaining ingredients; pour over hens. Cover and cook on low setting for 5 to 7 hours, basting once or twice with sauce in slow cooker, until juices run clear when pierced. Spoon sauce over hens to serve. Makes 2 servings.

Cheesy Chicken-Broccoli Quiche

Kendall Hale, Lynn, MA

2 lbs. boneless, skinless
  chicken breasts
10-oz. pkg. frozen chopped
  broccoli, thawed
3/4 c. all-purpose flour
3/4 t. baking powder
1/2 t. salt

1 c. evaporated milk
2 eggs
2 T. onion, chopped
2 t. dried parsley
1 c. shredded Cheddar
  cheese

Coat a slow cooker with non-stick vegetable spray. Arrange chicken in slow cooker; top with broccoli. Cover and cook on low setting for 6 to 8 hours, until chicken is fork-tender. In a bowl, whisk together flour, baking powder, salt, evaporated milk and eggs. Fold in remaining ingredients; pour mixture over broccoli. Increase heat to high; cover and cook for one hour, until set and cheese is melted. Serves 6.

Cheesy Chicken-Broccoli Quiche

Quick tip

Cut beef, chicken or pork into thin strips or slices in a snap! Just freeze the meat for 20 to 30 minutes before slicing.

Crockery Chicken Curry

Crockery Chicken Curry

Gracie Smith, British Columbia, Canada

1-1/2 lbs. boneless, skinless
  chicken thighs, cubed
2 carrots, peeled and sliced
1 onion, thinly sliced
2 T. cornstarch

4 t. curry powder
3/4 t. turmeric
salt and pepper to taste
1/2 head cauliflower, cut into
  flowerets

2 cloves garlic, minced
1/3 c. water
1-1/4 c. plain non-fat yogurt
1/4 c. fresh cilantro, chopped

Combine chicken, carrots and onion in a slow cooker. In a small bowl, stir together cornstarch and seasonings. Sprinkle cornstarch mixture over chicken mixture; toss to coat well. Add cauliflower, garlic and water to slow cooker. Cover and cook on low setting for 8 hours. Spoon one cup of juice from slow cooker into a bowl; stir in yogurt and cilantro. Stir yogurt mixture back into slow cooker. Serves 6.

Garlicky Bacon Chicken

Lisa Robason, Corpus Christi, TX

8 slices bacon
8 boneless, skinless chicken
  breasts

2 10-3/4 oz. cans cream of
  mushroom with roasted garlic
  soup

1 c. sour cream
1/2 c. all-purpose flour

Wrap one slice of bacon around each chicken breast and place in a slow cooker. In a medium bowl, whisk together soups, sour cream and flour. Pour over chicken. Cover and cook on low setting for 6 to 8 hours. Serves 8.

Creamy Italian Chicken & Noodles

Lynda Willoughby, Fort Mill, SC

6 boneless, skinless chicken thighs
2 1-oz. pkgs. zesty Italian salad
  dressing mix

32-oz. container chicken broth
2 8-oz. pkgs. cream cheese, cubed

16-oz. pkg. medium egg noodles,
  cooked

Place chicken thighs in a slow cooker. Sprinkle with dressing mix; pour broth over chicken. Cover and cook on low setting for 6 to 8 hours, until chicken is very tender. Remove chicken to a plate, reserving broth in a slow cooker; shred chicken with a fork and set aside. Add cream cheese to broth in slow cooker; stir until melted. Add cooked noodles and shredded chicken to slow cooker; stir gently. Let stand for about 15 minutes, until thickened and creamy. Makes 6 servings.

Shredded Buffalo Chicken Sliders

Nola Coons, Gooseberry Patch

4 boneless, skinless chicken
  breasts
1/4 c. cayenne hot pepper sauce

2/3 c. water
16 dinner rolls, split
1 c. blue cheese salad dressing

Garnish: celery sticks

Place chicken breasts in a lightly greased slow cooker. In a bowl, stir together hot sauce and water; drizzle over chicken. Cover and cook on low setting for 8 hours. Remove chicken and shred with 2 forks; return to sauce in slow cooker. To serve, place shredded chicken on bottom halves of rolls; evenly top with dressing. Replace tops of rolls. Serve with celery sticks. Serves 8.

Teriyaki Chicken Thighs

Beth Kramer, Port Saint Lucie, FL

1 onion, cut into thin wedges
20-oz. can pineapple cubes,
  drained
1 T. oil

8 chicken thighs, skin removed
1/2 t. salt
1/2 to 3/4 c. favorite teriyaki
  basting and glazing sauce

cooked rice
Garnish: sliced green onions,
  toasted sesame seed

Place onion and pineapple in a greased 4-quart slow cooker; set aside. Heat oil in a large skillet over medium heat. Add chicken; season with salt. Cook for about 4 minutes per side, until golden. Drain; add chicken to slow cooker. Spoon sauce over chicken. Cover and cook on low setting for 5 hours, or until chicken is no longer pink inside. Serve chicken, onion and pineapple over cooked rice, garnished as desired. Serves 4.

Chicken-Chili Con Queso Dip

Shannon Young, Churubusco, IN

2 boneless, skinless chicken
  breasts, cooked and shredded
32-oz. pkg. pasteurized process
  cheese spread, cubed

8-oz. pkg. cream cheese, cubed
16-oz. jar salsa
4-oz. can diced green chiles
tortilla chips

Combine all ingredients except tortilla chips in a slow cooker. Cover and cook on high setting for 1-1/2 to 2 hours, until cheese is melted, stirring occasionally. Reduce to low setting to serve. Serve with tortilla chips. Serves 12.

Shredded Buffalo Chicken Sliders

Quick tip

For easy, no-fuss cleaning, just fill an empty slow cooker with warm, soapy water and let soak.

Provincial Chicken

Provincial Chicken
Shari Upchurch, Dearing, GA

4 boneless, skinless chicken
  breasts
2 15-oz. cans diced
  tomatoes
2 zucchini, diced
10-3/4 oz. can cream of
  chicken soup
2 T. balsamic vinegar

1 T. dried, minced onion
2 T. dried parsley
1 t. dried basil
1 c. shredded Cheddar
  cheese
1/2 c. sour cream
  cooked bowtie pasta

In a slow cooker, combine chicken, tomatoes, zucchini, soup, vinegar, onion and herbs. Cover and cook on low setting for 6 to 8 hours. Remove chicken, cut into bite-size pieces and return to slow cooker. Stir in cheese and sour cream; cover and cook for an additional 15 minutes. To serve, spoon over cooked pasta. Serves 6.

French Country Chicken
Teri Lindquist, Gurnee, IL

1 onion, chopped
6 carrots, peeled and sliced
  diagonally
6 stalks celery, sliced
  diagonally
6 boneless, skinless chicken
  breasts
1 t. dried tarragon
1 t. dried thyme
pepper to taste

10-3/4 oz. can cream of
  chicken soup
1-1/2 oz. pkg. onion soup
  mix
1/3 c. dry white wine or
  chicken broth
2 T. cornstarch
  cooked rice or mashed
  potatoes

Combine onion, carrots and celery in the bottom of a slow cooker. Arrange chicken on top; sprinkle with seasonings. Mix together chicken soup and onion soup mix; spoon over chicken. Cover and cook on high setting for 4 hours, stirring after one hour. At serving time, stir together wine or broth and cornstarch; pour over chicken and mix well. Cook, uncovered, for an additional 10 minutes, or until thickened. Stir again; serve over cooked rice or mashed potatoes. Makes 6 servings.

Chicken Lasagna Florentine
Nicole Draves, Rockland, MA

10-oz. pkg. frozen chopped
  spinach, thawed and
  drained
9-oz. pkg. frozen diced
  cooked chicken, thawed
2 10-3/4 oz. cans cream of
  chicken soup
8-oz. container sour cream
1 c. milk
1/2 c. grated Parmesan
  cheese

1/3 c. onion, chopped
1/2 t. salt
1/4 t. pepper
1/8 t. nutmeg
9 strips lasagna, uncooked
  and divided
1 c. shredded mozzarella
  cheese, divided

Combine all ingredients except lasagna and mozzarella in a large bowl; stir well and set aside. Arrange 3 uncooked lasagna strips in the bottom of a slow cooker sprayed with non-stick vegetable spray, breaking strips in half to fit. Spread 1/3 of spinach mixture over lasagna; sprinkle with 1/3 cup mozzarella. Layer with 3 more strips, half of remaining spinach mixture and 1/3 cup mozzarella. Top with remaining lasagna strips, spinach mixture and mozzarella. Cover and cook on high setting for one hour. Reduce to low setting and cook, covered, for 5 hours, or until lasagna is tender. Makes 8 servings.

Midwest Chicken Sandwich

Linda Ketcham, Columbus, OH

50-oz. can dark and white
   chicken, drained and
   shredded
26-oz. can cream of
   chicken soup

salt and pepper to taste
24 sandwich buns, split
Optional: pickle slices

Mix chicken and soup in a slow cooker. Cover and cook on low setting for 3 to 4 hours. Add salt and pepper to taste; stir well. Spoon onto buns and garnish with pickle slices, if desired. Makes about 24 sandwiches.

Pineapple Chicken

Tonya Lewis, Crothersville, IN

6 boneless, skinless
   chicken breasts
salt, pepper and paprika to
   taste

20-oz. can pineapple
   tidbits, drained
2 T. Dijon mustard

Arrange chicken in a slow cooker; sprinkle with salt, pepper and paprika. Set aside. Mix together pineapple and mustard; spread over chicken. Cover and cook on high setting for 3 to 4 hours. Serves 6.

Creamed Chicken For a Crowd

Vickie

8 boneless, skinless
   chicken breasts, cubed
1 t. salt
1/2 t. pepper
2 to 4 T. olive oil, divided
2 white onions, chopped
6 carrots, peeled and
   thinly sliced

2 c. chicken broth, divided
2 to 3 sprigs fresh thyme
1/3 c. butter, softened
3 T. all-purpose flour
12 to 15 biscuits, split

Season chicken with salt and pepper. Heat one tablespoon oil in a skillet over medium heat. Working in batches, cook chicken until golden on all sides, adding another tablespoon of oil oil if needed. Remove chicken to a platter; set aside. Add remaining oil to skillet; cook onions in oil until translucent and lightly golden. Add chicken, carrots and one cup broth to onions. Stir gently and spoon chicken mixture into a lightly greased large slow cooker. Place thyme sprigs on top. Cover and cook on low setting for 5 to 6 hours, until chicken is nearly done. Discard thyme. In a small bowl, blend butter and flour. Add butter mixture and remaining broth to slow cooker; cook and stir until thickened. Increase heat to high; cover and cook for 30 minutes. Season with additional salt and pepper, if desired. To serve, ladle creamed chicken over split biscuits. Serves 12 to 15.

Midwest Chicken Sandwich

Quick side

Blend minced garlic, flavored cream cheese or shredded cheese into warm mashed potatoes for a delicious side dish.

Root Beer Pulled Pork Sandwiches

Simple Shredded Pork Tacos

Christine Horjus, Hebron, IN

2-lb. boneless pork loin
  roast
1 c. salsa
4-oz. can chopped green
  chiles
1/2 t. garlic salt

1/2 t. pepper
Optional: 7-1/2 oz. bottle
  mild taco sauce
8 10-inch flour tortillas,
  warmed

Combine all ingredients in a slow cooker except taco sauce and tortillas. Cover and cook on low setting for about 8 hours; drain juices. Shred pork and return to slow cooker. If desired, add taco sauce; heat through. Serve on tortillas. Makes 6 to 8 tacos.

Easy Slow-Cooker Burritos

Pam Schremmer, Wichita, KS

2-lb. pork loin, diced
26-oz. can chili beans
15-oz. can chili beans
16-oz. picante sauce
12 8-inch flour tortillas

Garnish: sour cream,
  shredded Cheddar
  cheese, sliced jalapeño
  peppers

Place pork, undrained beans and picante sauce in a slow cooker. Cover and cook on low setting for 8 hours. Spoon pork mixture into flour tortillas; garnish as desired. Serves 6.

Root Beer Pulled Pork Sandwiches

Sarah Gardner, Schuylerville, NY

2-lb. pork tenderloin
salt and pepper to taste
2 c. root beer

18-oz. bottle favorite
  barbecue sauce
5 to 6 potato rolls, split

Season pork on all sides with salt and pepper. Place pork in a slow cooker; pour root beer over top. Cover and cook on low setting for 4 to 6 hours, until pork is very tender. Remove pork from slow cooker and discard juices. Shred pork and return to slow cooker; stir in barbecue sauce. Serve pork on rolls for sandwiches. Serves 5 to 6.

Quick tip

Serve tacos or fajitas in a new way. Layer meat, lettuce and veggies in large clear plastic cups. Top with shredded cheese, chopped avocado and a dollop of sour cream. Provide sturdy plastic forks...guests can stroll and eat!

Teriyaki Pork Roast

Jodi Erdmann, Watertown, WI

3/4 c. apple juice
2 T. sugar
2 T. soy sauce
1 T. cider vinegar
1 t. ground ginger

1/4 t. garlic powder
1/8 t. pepper
2 to 3-lb. boneless center-cut
   rolled pork roast

1-1/2 T. cornstarch
3 T. cold water
Garnish: sliced green onions

Combine juice, sugar, soy sauce, vinegar and seasonings in a slow cooker; mix well. Add roast, turning to coat; place roast fat-side up. Cover and cook on low setting for 7 to 8 hours. Strain liquid into a small saucepan; bring to a boil. Mix together cornstarch and water in a small bowl; add to boiling liquid. Cook until thickened. Slice roast, serving gravy over top; sprinkle with green onions. Serves 4 to 6.

Chinese-Style BBQ Pork

Ruth Leonard, Columbus, OH

2-lb. boneless pork roast
1/4 c. soy sauce
1/4 c. hoisin sauce
3 T. catsup

3 T. honey
2 t. garlic, minced
2 t. fresh ginger, peeled and
   grated

1 t. dark sesame oil
1/2 t. Chinese 5-spice powder
1/2 c. chicken broth

Place roast in a large plastic zipping bag and set aside. In a small bowl, whisk together remaining ingredients except broth; pour over roast. Seal bag; refrigerate at least 2 hours, turning occasionally. Place roast in a slow cooker; pour marinade from bag over roast. Cover and cook on low setting for 8 hours. Remove pork from slow cooker; keep warm. Add broth to liquid in slow cooker; cover and cook on low setting for 30 minutes, or until thickened. Shred pork with 2 forks and stir into sauce in slow cooker. Serves 6.

Teriyaki Pork Roast

Saucy Ribs

Saucy Ribs

Zoe Bennett, Columbia, SC

1 t. dry mustard
1/2 t. allspice
1 t. salt
1 t. pepper

3 lbs. baby back pork ribs,
   sliced into 4-inch pieces
1/2 c. water
1-1/2 c. barbecue sauce

Combine all seasonings in a small bowl; rub onto ribs. Place in a slow cooker and pour water over top. Cover and cook on low setting for 8 to 9 hours, until ribs are tender when pierced with a fork. Remove ribs from slow cooker; discard cooking liquid. Replace ribs in slow cooker and add barbecue sauce. Cover and cook on low setting for one additional hour. Makes 6 servings.

Finger-Lickin' Ribs

Brad Daugherty, Columbus, OH

3 to 4 lbs. baby back pork
   ribs
salt and pepper to taste
garlic salt to taste

8-oz. bottle Russian salad
   dressing
3/4 c. pineapple juice

Slice ribs into several portions to fit into slow cooker; sprinkle with salt and pepper. Arrange in a slow cooker; add enough water just to cover. Cover and cook on high setting for 6 to 7 hours, until tender; drain. Arrange ribs on a broiler pan and sprinkle with garlic salt. Combine salad dressing and pineapple juice in a small mixing bowl; brush ribs with half the sauce. Broil until browned; turn over, brush with remaining sauce and broil other side. Serves 8 to 10.

Easy-Does-It Ribs

Jackie Lowe, Maysville, KY

3-1/2 to 4 lbs. country-style
   pork ribs

1 c. barbecue sauce
1 c. Catalina salad dressing

Spray a slow cooker with non-stick vegetable spray. Place ribs in slow cooker. Mix together barbecue sauce and salad dressing; pour over ribs. Cover and cook on low setting for 8 hours. Makes 6 to 8 servings.

Quick tip

A crockery bowl filled to the brim with ripe pears, apples and other fresh fruit makes an oh-so-simple centerpiece...it's an easy way to encourage healthy snacking too!

Hearty Red Beans & Rice

Tyson Ann Trecannelli, Fishing Creek, MD

16-oz. pkg. dried kidney beans
2 T. oil
1 onion, chopped
3 stalks celery, chopped
1 green pepper, chopped

2 cloves garlic, minced
3 c. water
2-2/3 c. beef broth
1/2 t. red pepper flakes
1 meaty ham bone or ham hock

1 t. salt
cooked rice
Garnish: chopped green onions,
    crisply cooked bacon

Soak beans overnight in enough water to cover; drain and set aside. In a large skillet, heat oil over medium-high heat. Add onion, celery, pepper and garlic; sauté until onion is translucent, 5 to 6 minutes. Place in a slow cooker along with drained beans, water, broth and red pepper flakes. Add ham bone and push down into mixture. Cover and cook on low setting until beans are very tender, 9 to 10 hours. Remove ham bone; dice meat and return to slow cooker. Stir in salt. Serve beans spooned over hot cooked rice in bowls. Garnish with green onions and bacon. Serves 6 to 8.

Swedish Cabbage Rolls

Arthur Cooper, Indio, CA

12 large leaves cabbage
1 egg, beaten
1/4 c. milk
1/2 c. onion, finely chopped

1 t. salt
1/4 t. pepper
1 lb. ground pork
1 c. cooked rice

8-oz. can tomato sauce
1 T. lemon juice
1 t. Worcestershire sauce
Garnish: sour cream

Cook cabbage leaves in a large kettle of boiling water for 3 to 5 minutes, or until limp; drain well and set aside. Combine egg, milk, onion, salt, pepper, pork and cooked rice; mix well. Place about 1/4 cup meat mixture in the center of each leaf; fold in sides and roll ends over meat. Arrange cabbage rolls in a slow cooker. Combine remaining ingredients and pour over rolls. Cover and cook on low setting for 7 to 9 hours. Spoon sauce over rolls and garnish with sour cream. Makes 6 servings.

Swedish Cabbage Rolls

Quick tip

It's easy to get more veggies into your family's meals. Keep frozen vegetable blends on hand to toss into mac & cheese, soups and casseroles.

Mike's Irresistible Italian Chops

Mike's Irresistible Italian Chops

Leslie McKinley, Macomb, MO

5 pork chops
1-1/2 onions, coarsely
  chopped
15-oz. can stewed tomatoes
1/3 c. oil
1-1/2 t. Italian seasoning

1-1/2 t. garlic powder
2 t. smoke-flavored
  cooking sauce
1/4 c. water
cooked couscous

Layer chops and onions in a slow cooker; add tomatoes with juice and remaining ingredients except couscous. Cover and cook on low setting for 3 to 4 hours, until chops are tender. Serve over couscous. Makes 5 servings.

French Onion Pork Chops

Rebecca Ruff, Carthage, NY

4 pork chops
10-1/2 oz. can French
  onion soup

1/4 c. water
1 t. dried parsley
cooked egg noodles

Place pork chops in a slow cooker. Mix soup and water together; pour over pork. Sprinkle with parsley. Cover and cook on low for about 8 hours. Serve over hot cooked noodles. Serves 4.

Oktoberfest Pork Roast

Sherry Doherty, Medford, NJ

3 to 4-lb. boneless pork
  roast
salt and pepper to taste
1 T. shortening
2 apples, peeled, cored and
  quartered

32-oz. pkg. sauerkraut
1 c. apple juice or water
Optional: 17-oz. pkg.
  fresh or frozen pierogies

Sprinkle roast with salt and pepper. Melt shortening in a skillet over high heat; brown roast on all sides. Place roast in slow cooker. Add apples, sauerkraut and juice or water; blend. Add pierogies, if using; push down gently to partially submerge them in the liquid. Cover and cook on low setting for 8 to 9 hours. Serves 4 to 6.

Creole Shrimp & Sausage

Kerry Mayer, Dunham Springs, LA

1 onion, chopped
1 green pepper, chopped
2 stalks celery, sliced
2 carrots, peeled and diced
4 cloves garlic, minced

14-1/2 oz. can diced tomatoes
3/4 c. chicken broth
2 t. Creole seasoning
3 andouille pork sausage links,
  cut into 1/2-inch pieces

10-oz. pkg. frozen corn, thawed
1 T. tomato paste
1 lb. large shrimp, peeled and
  cleaned
cooked rice

In a large bowl, combine onion, pepper, celery, carrots, garlic, tomatoes with juice, broth and seasoning. Mix well; stir in sausage and corn. Add mixture to a lightly greased slow cooker. Cover and cook on low setting for 8 hours. Stir in tomato paste and shrimp. Cover and cook for 7 to 10 more minutes, until shrimp is cooked. Spoon over rice to serve. Serves 6.

Easy Kielbasa Supper

Victoria Landry, Shirley, MA

1 yellow onion, sliced
32-oz. jar sauerkraut, drained
  and rinsed

4 to 5 whole peppercorns
Optional: 1 t. caraway seed
4 to 5 potatoes, quartered

1-lb. Kielbasa pork sausage

In a slow cooker, layer onion slices and sauerkraut; sprinkle with peppercorns and caraway seed, if using. Add potatoes; place sausage link on top. Cover and cook on high setting for 4 hours. Remove sausage link from crock and slice to serve; stir remaining vegetables to mix. Makes 5 to 6 servings.

Quick side

Cool coleslaw is always a welcome partner to spicy dishes. Mix up bagged shredded cabbage mix with bottled coleslaw dressing to taste, then make it special with diced apple or even crumbled blue cheese. Ready in a jiffy!

Easy Kielbasa Supper

Quick side

Baked potatoes are tasty with any dish, and with a slow cooker, so easy to prepare. Simply use a fork to pierce 10 to 12 baking potatoes and wrap each in aluminum foil. Arrange them in a slow cooker, cover and cook on high setting for 2-1/2 to 4 hours, until tender.

Savory Slow-Cooked Pork Loin

Colorado Pork Chops

Linda Wolfe, Westminster, CO

6 bone-in pork chops, 1-1/2 inches
  thick
15-oz. can chili beans with chili
  sauce

1-1/2 c. salsa
1 c. corn
Optional: green chiles to taste
  cooked rice

Garnish: chopped fresh cilantro

In a slow cooker, layer pork chops, beans, salsa, corn and chiles, if using. Cover and cook on low setting for 5 hours, or on high setting for 2-1/2 hours. Serve over cooked rice; garnish with cilantro. Serves 6.

Savory Slow-Cooked Pork Loin

Kathleen Hendrick, Alexandria, KY

2-lb. pork loin, quartered
1.2-oz. pkg. brown gravy mix
1 c. water
1 c. apple juice
1/2 c. applesauce

2 t. Worcestershire sauce
1 stalk celery, sliced into 1/2-inch
  pieces
1 onion, chopped
1-1/2 t. seasoned salt

1/2 t. pepper
Optional: 1 T. cornstarch,
  1 T. water

Place pork in a slow cooker. In a bowl, combine gravy mix and water; stir until dissolved. Add remaining ingredients except optional cornstarch and water to gravy mixture; mix well. Spoon gravy mixture over pork. Cover and cook on low setting for 8 hours, or until pork is very tender. If liquid in slow cooker needs to be thickened, whisk together cornstarch and one tablespoon water in a cup. Stir into slow cooker during the last 30 minutes of cooking. Serves 4 to 6.

Kickin' Pork Chops

Amy Woods, Collinsville, TX

4 to 6 thick-cut boneless pork
  chops
10-3/4 oz. can cream of chicken
  soup

1-oz. pkg. ranch salad dressing
  mix

1 T. Creole seasoning

Spray a slow cooker with non-stick cooking spray. Lay pork chops in slow cooker and set aside. Mix remaining ingredients in a bowl; spoon over pork chops. Cover and cook on low setting for 4 to 5 hours, until pork chops are tender. Makes 4 to 6 servings.

Prize-Winning *Pork*

Slow-Cooker Cola Ham

Elsie Mellinger, Annville, PA

3 to 4-lb. fully cooked ham
1/2 c. brown sugar, packed
1 t. dry mustard
12-oz. can cola

Place ham in a slow cooker. Combine brown sugar and mustard; stir in enough cola to make a glaze consistency. Pour glaze over ham, coating well. Cover and cook on low setting for 8 to 10 hours, basting occasionally with juices. Serves 8 to 10.

Ginger Beer Spareribs

Katie Contario, Centreville, VA

3 lbs. center-cut pork spareribs, halved
3 12-oz. bottles ginger beer
36-oz. bottle catsup
2 c. water

Combine all ingredients in a slow cooker. Cover and cook on low setting for 8 hours. If sauce is too thin, increase slow cooker to high setting for 30 minutes. Serves 4 to 6.

Un-Cola Pulled Pork

Debi Hodges, Frederica, DE

1 onion, quartered and halved
2-1/2 to 3-lb. pork shoulder or butt roast
1/4 c. cider vinegar
3 T. Worcestershire sauce
2 12-oz. cans lemon-lime soda
2 cloves garlic, minced
1-1/2 t. dry mustard
1/4 t. cayenne pepper
salt and pepper to taste
1 to 2 c. favorite barbecue sauce

Place onion in a slow cooker; top with roast. Sprinkle with vinegar, Worcestershire sauce, soda, garlic and seasonings. Cover and cook on low setting for 7 to 8 hours, or on high setting for 4 to 5 hours, until pork is tender. Remove roast to a large cutting board; shred with 2 forks. Return shredded pork to slow cooker; cover and cook for one additional hour. Drain cooking liquid in slow cooker. Add desired amount of barbecue sauce to pork and onion mixture. Heat through. Makes 6 to 8 servings.

Slow-Cooker Cola Ham

Apple Butter BBQ Spareribs

Apple-Glazed Pork Roast

Rogene Rogers, Bemidji, MN

4-lb. pork loin roast
salt and pepper to taste
6 apples, quartered and
   cored
1/4 c. apple juice
3 T. brown sugar,
   packed
1 t. ground ginger

Season roast on all sides with salt and pepper. Place roast on a baking sheet and brown on both sides under a broiler. Arrange apples in a slow cooker; top with roast. In a bowl, whisk together juice, brown sugar and ginger; drizzle over roast. Cover and cook on high setting for 6 hours, or until roast is no longer pink in the center and apples are tender. Serves 8 to 10.

Apple Butter BBQ Spareribs

Catherine Rivard, Moline, IL

4 lbs. pork spareribs
salt and pepper to taste
16-oz. jar apple butter
18-oz. bottle barbecue
   sauce
1 onion, quartered

Sprinkle ribs with salt and pepper. Place ribs on rimmed baking sheets. Bake at 350 degrees for 30 minutes; drain. Meanwhile, blend together apple butter and barbecue sauce in a bowl; set aside. Slice ribs into serving-size pieces and place in a slow cooker. Top with onion; drizzle sauce mixture over all. Cover and cook on low setting for 8 hours. Makes 4 to 6 servings.

Apple Orchard Pork Roast

Marion Sundberg, Ramona, CA

2-lb. pork shoulder
   roast
1 T. oil
2 tart apples, peeled,
   cored and sliced
8 new redskin potatoes
1 onion, coarsely
   chopped
16-oz. pkg. baby carrots
10-3/4 oz. can cream of
   celery or mushroom
   soup
Worcestershire sauce to
   taste
salt and pepper to taste

Brown pork roast in oil on all sides; place in a slow cooker. Add apples and vegetables; top with remaining ingredients. Cover and cook on low setting for 7 to 8 hours, until roast is cooked through. Arrange meat and vegetables on a platter. Serve with cooking juices, thickened in a saucepan on the stove if needed. Makes 6 servings.

Quick side

Make herbed butter to serve with dinner in a jiffy...just roll a stick of butter in freshly chopped herbs, slice and serve!

Pintos & Pork Over Corn Chips

Susan Butters, Bountiful, UT

16-oz. pkg. dried pinto
  beans
3-lb. pork loin roast
7 c. water
4-oz. can chopped green
  chiles
1/2 c. onion, chopped
2 cloves garlic, minced
2 T. chili powder

1 T. ground cumin
1 T. salt
1 t. oregano
Garnish: corn chips,
  sour cream, shredded
  Cheddar cheese, chopped
  tomatoes, shredded
  lettuce

Cover beans with water in a large soup pot; soak
overnight. Drain. Add beans and remaining ingredients
except garnish to a slow cooker. Cover and cook on low
setting for 9 hours; remove meat from bones and return
to slow cooker. Cook, uncovered, for 30 minutes or until
thickened. Serve over corn chips, garnished as desired.
Serves 10.

Pork Sandwich Spread

Janie Reed, Zanesville, OH

2 to 3-lb. pork roast
1/4 t. dried basil
1/4 t. dried oregano
salt and pepper to taste

3 eggs
1 sleeve round buttery
  crackers
20 sandwich buns, split

Place roast in a slow cooker; sprinkle with seasonings.
Cover and cook on high setting for 2 to 3 hours, until
fork-tender. Remove roast; cool. Reserve 1/2 cup cooking
liquid. Grind meat with a meat grinder; add eggs and
crushed crackers. Add reserved liquid and enough water
to obtain consistency of thick soup. Return meat mixture
to slow cooker and cook on low setting for an additional
2 hours. Spoon onto warm buns. Makes 20 sandwiches.

Calico Beans

Molly Wilson, Rapid City, SD

1/2 lb. bacon, crisply
  cooked and crumbled
32-oz. can pork & beans
16-oz. can corn, drained
16-oz. can lima beans,
  drained and rinsed

16-oz. can kidney beans,
  drained and rinsed
2 onions, chopped
3/4 c. brown sugar, packed
1 c. catsup
1 t. mustard

Combine bacon, pork & beans, corn and beans in a slow
cooker; set aside. Stir together remaining ingredients;
add to slow cooker and mix well. Cover and cook on low
setting for 4 to 6 hours. Serves 10 to 12.

Quick tip

To get a slow cooker to work its best,
always fill it from 1/2 to 2/3 full of
recipe ingredients

Pork Sandwich Spread

Sweet & Spicy Country-Style Ribs

Sweet & Spicy Country-Style Ribs

Kandy Bingham, Green River, WY

2 to 3 lbs. bone-in country-style
pork ribs, sliced into serving-size
pieces
1 onion, sliced

salt and pepper to taste
18-oz. bottle favorite barbecue
sauce

1/2 c. maple syrup
1/4 c. spicy brown mustard

Place ribs in a slow cooker that has been sprayed with non-stick vegetable spray. Place onion on top of ribs; sprinkle with salt and pepper. In a bowl, mix together remaining ingredients; pour over all. Cover and cook on low setting for 8 to 10 hours. Makes 4 to 6 servings.

Country-Style Ribs & Redskins

Audrey Lett, Newark, DE

3 lbs. country-style pork ribs
1-1/2 lbs. new redskin potatoes

salt and pepper to taste
27-oz. can sauerkraut

Arrange ribs in a slow cooker; top with potatoes. Sprinkle with salt and pepper; spoon in sauerkraut. Cover and cook on low setting for 7 to 9 hours. Add salt and pepper to taste before serving, as needed. Serves 6.

Maple Whiskey Ribs

Staci Allen, Sheboygan, WI

1/2 c. pure maple syrup
1/4 c. whiskey or fruit juice
2 T. Dijon mustard

2 lbs. pork spareribs, cut into
serving-size sections

1 purple onion, sliced

In a small bowl, whisk together syrup, whiskey or juice and mustard. Brush mixture over spareribs. Place ribs in a slow cooker; top with onion slices. Cover and cook on low setting for 6 to 8 hours, until ribs are very tender. Makes 4 servings.

Super-Easy Sausage Sandwiches

Beth Harman, Hegins, PA

1-1/2 lbs. Italian pork sausage links
2 green peppers, sliced
1 onion, sliced

24-oz. can spaghetti sauce
pepper to taste
6 to 8 sandwich rolls, split

Place sausage links in a slow cooker. Layer peppers and onion over links; spoon sauce over all. Season with pepper. Cover and cook on low setting for 6 hours. Place sausages in rolls and top with peppers, onions and sauce from slow cooker. Serves 6 to 8.

County Fair Italian Sausages

Dale Duncan, Waterloo, IA

20-oz. pkg. Italian pork sausage links
1 green pepper, sliced
1 onion, sliced

26-oz. jar spaghetti sauce
5 sub buns, split
Garnish: 5 slices Provolone cheese

Brown sausages in a non-stick skillet over medium heat; place in a slow cooker. Add pepper and onion; top with sauce. Cover and cook on low setting for 4 to 6 hours. To serve, place sausages in buns; top with sauce mixture and cheese. Makes 5 sandwiches.

Aloha Sausage Links

Barb Stout, Columbus, OH

2 lbs. smoked pork sausage links, sliced 1/2-inch thick
8-oz. bottle Catalina salad dressing

8-oz. bottle Russian salad dressing
1/2 c. brown sugar, packed
1/2 c. pineapple juice

Brown sausage in a skillet over medium heat; drain and place in a slow cooker. Add dressings, sugar and juice to skillet; cook and stir over medium-low heat until sugar is dissolved. Pour over sausage. Cover and cook on low setting for one to 2 hours. Makes 16 servings.

Quick tip

Keep bugs away from your cool glasses of lemonade...simply poke a hole through a paper cupcake liner, add a straw, flip it upside-down and use it as a beverage cap. So clever!

Country Fair Italian Sausages

Kielbasa & Red Beans

Quick tip

The ceramic insert in a slow cooker may crack if exposed to abrupt temperature shifts. Don't set a hot crock directly on a cold counter; always put a tea towel down first. Likewise, don't put a crock straight from the refrigerator into a preheated base.

Kielbasa & Red Beans

Beth Schlieper, Lakewood, CO

1 lb. Kielbasa, cut into bite-size
  pieces
4 to 5 16-oz. cans red beans,
  drained and rinsed

2 14-1/2 oz. cans diced tomatoes
1 onion, chopped
hot pepper sauce to taste

Combine all ingredients in a slow cooker. Cover and cook on low setting for 8 hours, or on high setting for 4 to 5 hours. Serves 6 to 8.

Hearty Pork & Beans

Pam Hundley, Port Crane, NY

1 lb. ground beef
1 green pepper, chopped
1 onion, chopped
16-oz. pkg. smoked pork sausage,
  halved lengthwise and thinly
  sliced

16-oz. can pork & beans
15-oz. can lima beans, drained
  and rinsed
15-oz. can pinto beans, drained
  and rinsed
1 c. catsup

1/2 c. brown sugar, packed
1 t. salt
1/2 t. garlic powder
1/4 t. pepper

In a skillet over medium heat, brown beef with green pepper and onion; drain. Add remaining ingredients to a lightly greased slow cooker; stir in beef mixture. Cover and cook on low setting for 4 to 5 hours, until heated through. Serves 8.

Meatloaf Made Easy

Aleta Mottet, Fairfield, IA

1 lb. ground pork sausage
1 lb. lean ground beef
1 onion, finely diced
2 c. shredded mozzarella
  cheese
1 c. dry bread crumbs
1 egg
1/2 c. milk
salt and pepper to taste
1 c. catsup
1/2 c. brown sugar

In a bowl, combine all ingredients except catsup and brown sugar. Form mixture into a rounded loaf. Place in a slow cooker; poke a few holes in the top of meatloaf with a skewer. In a bowl, stir together catsup and brown sugar. Spoon mixture over meatloaf. Cover and cook on low setting for 3 to 5 hours, until meatloaf is no longer pink in the center. Serves 6 to 8.

Spaghetti Sauce with Italian Sausage

Amy Fehlberg, Allison, IA

1 T. olive oil
6 Italian pork sausage
  links
1 c. green pepper, chopped
1 onion, chopped
2 cloves garlic, sliced
28-oz. can crushed
  tomatoes
2 8-oz. cans tomato sauce
6-oz. can tomato paste
1/4 c. sugar
1 T. dried basil
1 T. dried oregano
1 T. Italian seasoning
salt and pepper to taste
cooked ziti pasta

Heat oil in a skillet over medium heat. Brown sausages with green pepper, onion and garlic. Add tomatoes with juice and remaining ingredients except pasta to a slow cooker; mix well. Spoon sausage mixture into tomato mixture in slow cooker. Cover and cook on low setting for 6 hours. Serve sausages and sauce over cooked pasta. Serves 8 to 10.

Louisiana Sausage Sandwiches

Dana Cunningham, Lafayette, LA

19.76-oz. pkg. Italian pork
  sausage links
1 green pepper, sliced into
  bite-size pieces
1 onion, sliced into
  bite-size pieces
8-oz. can tomato sauce
1/8 t. pepper
6 hoagie rolls, split

In a large skillet, brown sausage links over medium heat. Cut into 1/2-inch slices; place in a slow cooker. Stir in remaining ingredients except rolls. Cover and cook on low setting for 8 hours. Spoon onto rolls with a slotted spoon. Makes 6 sandwiches.

Spaghetti Sauce with Italian Sausage

Smoky Hobo Dinner

🥄🍴 *Quick tip*

Keep camping meals easy with one-skillet and one-pot recipes. Don't forget to pack a slow cooker in the RV too...dinner will practically cook itself!

Smoky Hobo Dinner

Julie Pak, Henryetta, OK

5 potatoes, peeled and quartered
1 head cabbage, coarsely chopped
16-oz. pkg. baby carrots
1 onion, thickly sliced

salt and pepper to taste
14-oz. pkg. smoked pork sausage,
　sliced into 2-inch pieces

1/2 c. water

Spray a slow cooker with non-stick vegetable spray. Layer vegetables in slow cooker in order listed, sprinkling each layer with salt and pepper. Place sausage on top of vegetables in slow cooker; pour water over all. Cover and cook on low setting for 6 to 8 hours. Serves 6.

Brunswick Stew

Jennie Gist, Gooseberry Patch

3-lb. boneless pork shoulder roast,
　quartered
3 redskin potatoes, diced
1 onion, chopped
28-oz. can crushed tomatoes

18-oz. bottle favorite barbecue
　sauce
14-oz. can chicken broth
9-oz. pkg. frozen baby lima beans,
　thawed

9-oz. pkg. frozen corn, thawed
6 T. brown sugar, packed
1 t. salt
Garnish: saltine crackers

Stir together all ingredients except crackers in a slow cooker. Cover and cook on high setting for 6 hours, or until pork and potatoes are tender. Remove pork with a slotted spoon; shred. Return pork to slow cooker; stir well. Ladle stew into bowls; serve with crackers. Serves 6.

Eleanor's Lentil Stew

Eleanor Paternoster, Bridgeport, CT

16-oz. pkg. dried lentils
4 c. water

3 c. cooked ham, diced
2 c. celery, chopped

2 c. carrots, peeled and chopped
2 10-1/2 oz. cans chicken broth

Combine all ingredients in a slow cooker. Cover and cook on low setting for 7 to 9 hours. Serves 8.

German Roast Pork & Sauerkraut

Sherry Doherty, Medford, NJ

3 to 4-lb. boneless pork roast
salt and pepper to taste
1 T. shortening

32-oz. pkg. sauerkraut
2 apples, peeled, cored and
   quartered

1 c. apple juice or water
14-oz. pkg. frozen pierogies

Sprinkle roast with salt and pepper. Heat shortening in a skillet over medium-high heat. Brown roast on all sides; place in a slow cooker. Add undrained sauerkraut, apples and juice or water; blend. Gently add pierogies so they are partly submerged in the sauerkraut (as the roast cooks, more liquid will cover the pierogies). Cover and cook on low setting for 8 to 9 hours. Serves 4 to 6.

Old-Fashioned Pork & Sauerkraut

Sharon Golden, Shamokin, PA

2 32-oz. pkgs. sauerkraut
2 c. water

salt and pepper to taste
3-lb. boneless pork tenderloin

Place sauerkraut with juice in a slow cooker. Drizzle water over sauerkraut; season with salt and pepper. Place pork on top of sauerkraut mixture; season with salt and pepper again, if preferred. Cover and cook on low setting for 8 to 10 hours, until pork is very tender. Serves 6 to 8.

Polish Sausage & Cabbage Soup

Marcia Shaffer, Conneaut Lake, PA

1-1/4 to 1-1/2 lbs. smoked
   Polish pork sausage links, halved
   lengthwise and sliced 1/2-inch
   thick

4 c. fat-free chicken broth
4 c. cabbage, chopped
2 c. potatoes, peeled and cubed
1 to 2 onions, chopped

1 carrot peeled and shredded
2 T. caraway seed, crushed
salt and pepper to taste

Combine all ingredients in a slow cooker. Cover and cook on low setting for 7 to 8 hours. Makes 6 to 8 servings.

Quick tip

When toting a slow-cooker dish to a potluck, wrap a rubber band around one handle, bring it up over the lid and secure it over the other handle...the lid stays on nice and tight!

German Roast Pork & Sauerkraut

Pork Chop à la Orange

Pork Chops à la Orange

Rogene Rogers, Bemidji, MN

3 lbs. pork chops
salt and pepper
2 c. orange juice
2 11-oz. cans mandarin
  oranges, drained

8-oz. can pineapple tidbits,
  drained
cooked egg noodles

Sprinkle pork chops with salt and pepper; place in a slow cooker. Pour orange juice over pork. Cover and cook on low setting for 6 to 8 hours, or on high setting for 3 to 4 hours. About 30 minutes before serving, add oranges and pineapple; continue cooking just until warm. Serve with cooked noodles. Serves 6 to 8.

Pork Chops & Scalloped Potatoes

Barb Sulser, Delaware, OH

1 onion, sliced, separated
  into rings and divided
8 potatoes, peeled, sliced
  and divided
16-oz. pkg. pasteurized
  process cheese spread,
  sliced and divided

6 boneless pork chops
salt and pepper to taste
10-3/4 oz. can cream of
  chicken soup

Spread a layer of onion rings in a slow cooker. Place a layer of potatoes over onion rings, then a layer of cheese. Continue to layer until slow cooker is two-thirds full. Sprinkle pork chops with salt and pepper; place on top. Spread soup over top. Cover and cook on low setting for 6 to 8 hours, or on high setting for 3 to 4 hours.

Pork Chops & Tomato Rice

Janice Hardin, Lincoln, NE

4 pork chops
1 T. oil
1 to 2 t. oil
salt and pepper to taste
10-3/4 oz. can tomato soup
3/4 c. long-cooking rice,
  uncooked

1 c. boiling water
1/3 c. onion, finely
  chopped
1/3 c. green pepper,
  chopped
1/4 t. Worcestershire sauce
1/2 t. salt

In a skillet over medium heat, brown pork chops in oil. Season with salt and pepper; place in a slow cooker. Combine remaining ingredients in a bowl; spoon evenly over pork chops. Cover and cook on low setting for 6 to 8 hours. Add a little more water if mixture gets too dry. Makes 4 servings.

Prize-Winning *Pork*

Savory Pork Carnitas

Lisa Wagner, Delaware, OH

3 to 4-lb. Boston butt pork roast
1-1/4 oz. pkg. taco seasoning mix
3 cloves garlic, sliced
1 onion, quartered
4-oz. can green chiles, drained

3/4 to 1 c. water
6 to 8 flour tortillas
Garnish: shredded lettuce, chopped tomatoes, sliced avocado, sour cream, lime wedges, sliced green onions, fresh cilantro sprigs

Combine pork, taco seasoning, garlic, onion and chiles in a slow cooker. Add water, using the full amount if pork is closer to 4 pounds; stir to combine. Cover and cook for 10 hours on low setting, or 6 hours on high setting, until tender enough to shred. Spoon shredded pork down center of tortillas and serve with desired garnishes. Makes 8 servings.

BBQ Pulled-Pork Fajitas

Jackie Valvardi, Haddon Heights, NJ

2-1/2 lb. boneless pork loin roast, trimmed
1 onion, thinly sliced
2 c. barbecue sauce
3/4 c. chunky salsa
1 T. chili powder

1 t. ground cumin
16-oz. pkg. frozen stir-fry peppers and onions
1/2 t. salt
18 8 to 10-inch flour tortillas, warmed

Place roast in a slow cooker; top with onion. Mix sauce, salsa and spices; pour over roast. Cover and cook on low setting for 8 to 10 hours. Remove roast and place on a cutting board; shred, using 2 forks. Return to slow cooker and mix well; add stir-fry vegetables and salt. Increase setting to high; cover and cook for an additional 30 minutes, until hot and vegetables are tender. With a slotted spoon, fill each warmed tortilla with 1/2 cup pork mixture. Makes 18 servings.

Easy Carnitas

Christine Arrieta, Aurora, CO

4 to 5-lb. boneless pork shoulder butt roast
seasoned meat tenderizer, salt and pepper to taste
2 T. olive oil

1/2 onion, chopped
2 cloves garlic, minced
28-oz. can green enchilada sauce

Sprinkle roast generously with tenderizer, salt and pepper; set aside. Heat oil in a large skillet over medium heat. Sauté onion for 2 minutes, or just until translucent. Add garlic; cook for one additional minute. Push onion and garlic to edge of skillet; add roast and brown on all sides. Transfer roast to a large slow cooker; top with onion mixture and enchilada sauce. Cover and cook on low setting for 8 hours, or on high setting for 3 hours, until pork is fork-tender. Shred roast with 2 forks; serve as desired in tacos, burritos and on nachos. Makes 10 to 12 servings.

Quick tip

If you love super-spicy chili, give New Mexico chili powder a try. Sold at Hispanic and specialty food stores, it contains pure ground red chili peppers, unlike regular chili powder which is a blend of chili, garlic and other seasonings.

BBQ Pulled-Pork Fajitas

Honey-Mustard Pork Tenderloin

Honey-Mustard Pork Tenderloin

Tammy Griffin, Ontario, Canada

2 1-lb. pork tenderloins	2 T. brown sugar, packed
salt and pepper to taste	1 T. cider vinegar
1 clove garlic, minced	1/2 t. dried thyme
1/4 c. Dijon mustard	1 T. cornstarch
2 T. honey	1 T. cold water

Season pork on all sides with salt and pepper. Place pork in a slow cooker; set aside. In a bowl, combine garlic, mustard, honey, brown sugar, vinegar and thyme; drizzle over pork. Turn pork to coat thoroughly. Cover and cook on low setting for 7 to 9 hours, until pork is very tender. Remove pork to a serving plate; keep warm. Pour juices from slow cooker into a saucepan; bring to a boil over medium heat. Reduce heat and simmer for 8 to 10 minutes, until slightly reduced. Combine cornstarch and water; whisk into juices. Cook until thickened, about 2 to 4 minutes. Slice pork and serve with gravy from saucepan. Serves 4 to 6.

Sweet & Tangy Pork Roast

Carol Lytle, Columbus, OH

2-1/2 lb. boneless pork shoulder roast	1/2 c. cranberry juice cocktail, divided
1 c. sweetened dried cranberries	1/2 t. salt
1/2 c. chicken broth	1/8 t. pepper
	2 T. cornstarch

Place roast in a slow cooker. Combine cranberries, broth, 1/4 cup juice, salt and pepper in a small bowl; pour over roast. Cover and cook on low setting for 7 to 9 hours. Remove roast; cover with aluminum foil to keep warm. Pour juices from slow cooker into a medium saucepan. Combine remaining juice with cornstarch in a small bowl; mix well. Stir into juices in saucepan; cook and stir over medium heat until thickened and bubbly, about 3 minutes. Serve with roast. Makes 6 servings.

Cuban-Style Pork Roast

Shannon Molden, Hermiston, OR

2 T. olive oil	3 to 4 cloves garlic, minced
2 t. ground cumin	2 T. lime juice
2 t. dried oregano	2 T. orange juice
1 T. salt	3 to 3-1/2 lb. boneless pork shoulder
1 t. pepper	cooked rice
1/2 t. red pepper flakes	

In a small bowl, mix together oil, seasonings, garlic and juices; set aside. Pierce pork roast all over with a fork; place in a slow cooker. Pour oil mixture over pork; turn to coat well. Cover and cook on low setting for 5 to 6 hours, turning halfway through, until pork is very tender. Remove pork from slow cooker; shred with 2 forks. Return shredded pork to juices in slow cooker; mix well. To serve, spoon pork and some juices from slow cooker over rice. Serves 6 to 8.

Quick tip

Look for apple cider vinegar at autumn farmstands. It's useful in so many ways like pickling and making salad dressing. Add a splash to cooked vegetables or a dash to skillet drippings when making gravy.

Garlicky Herbed Pork Roast

Nancy Wise, Little Rock, AR

4 to 5-lb. pork roast	1/2 t. dried sage	1 t. lemon zest
4 cloves garlic, slivered	1/2 t. ground cloves	2 T. cold water
1 t. dried thyme	1 t. salt	2 T. cornstarch

Cut 16 small pockets into roast with a knife tip; insert garlic slivers. Combine seasonings and zest; rub over roast. Place roast in a slow cooker. Cover and cook on low setting for 7 to 9 hours, or on high setting for 4 to 5 hours. Allow roast to stand 10 to 15 minutes before slicing. Remove and discard garlic pieces. Strain juices into a saucepan over medium heat; bring to a boil. Mix together water and cornstarch until dissolved; gradually add to saucepan. Cook until thickened, about 5 minutes. Serve gravy over sliced pork. Serves 8 to 10.

Pork Loin Roast & Gravy

Leslie McMahon, Houston, TX

4 to 5-lb. pork loin end roast, tied with kitchen string	2 onions, sliced	2 T. cornstarch
salt and pepper to taste	1 bay leaf	2 T. cold water
1 clove garlic, thinly sliced	1 c. hot water	
	2 T. Worcestershire sauce	

Season roast on all sides with salt and pepper. Cut tiny slits into roast with a knife tip; insert thin slices of garlic into slits. Arrange one sliced onion in the bottom of a slow cooker; top with roast. Place remaining sliced onion on top of roast; add remaining ingredients except cornstarch and water. Cover and cook on low setting for 8 to 10 hours, until roast is very tender. Remove roast and onions to a serving platter; discard bay leaf. In a cup, combine cornstarch and water; whisk into juices in slow cooker. Increase heat to high setting and cook gravy for about 15 minutes, until thickened. Serve roast and onions drizzled with gravy. Serves 8.

Garlicky Herbed Pork Roast

Pineapple-Cranberry Pork Roast

Autumn Pork Roast

Vickie

2-lb. boneless pork loin roast
3/4 t. salt
1/4 t. pepper
2 c. apple cider, divided

3 sprigs fresh rosemary, divided
1/2 c. sweetened dried cherries
5 t. cornstarch

Sprinkle roast with salt and pepper; place in a non-stick skillet coated with non-stick vegetable spray. Brown roast over medium heat for about 4 minutes per side. Pour one cup apple cider into a slow cooker. Add 2 sprigs rosemary; top with roast and remaining rosemary. Sprinkle cherries around roast. Cover and cook on low setting for 5 to 6 hours, or until a meat thermometer reads 160 degrees. Remove roast; keep warm. Strain cooking juices into a small saucepan. Stir in 3/4 cup cider; bring to a boil over medium heat. Combine remaining cider and cornstarch until smooth. Gradually whisk into cider mixture. Bring to a boil; cook and stir for one to 2 minutes, until thickened. Serve over roast. Makes 6 servings.

Fruited Roast Pork

Melody Taynor, Everett, WA

1 onion, sliced
2-lb. boneless pork loin roast
7-oz. pkg. mixed dried fruit, coarsely chopped

3/4 c. apple cider
1/2 t. nutmeg
1/4 t. cinnamon
1/2 t. salt

Place onion slices in the bottom of a slow cooker. Add roast; top with fruit. Mix remaining ingredients in a cup; drizzle over roast. Cover and cook on low setting for 6 to 8 hours, until pork is tender. Remove roast to a serving platter; let stand several minutes before slicing. Serve sliced roast topped with fruit sauce from slow cooker. Serves 6 to 8.

Pineapple-Cranberry Pork Roast

Carrie Kelderman, Pella, IA

3-lb. pork loin roast
20-oz. can crushed pineapple
1.35-oz. pkg. onion soup mix

1 c. sweetened dried cranberries
2 T. all-purpose flour
3 T. water

Place roast in a slow cooker. In a bowl, mix together pineapple with juice, soup mix and cranberries; spoon mixture over roast. Cover and cook on low setting for 8 hours. Remove roast to a serving platter and increase heat to high setting. In a cup, mix together flour and water; whisk into juices in slow cooker. Cook for 15 minutes, or until gravy has thickened. Serve pork drizzled with gravy from slow cooker. Serves 6 to 8.

South-of-the-Border Breakfast

Jo Ann

1 lb. ground pork breakfast
  sausage, browned and drained
4-oz. can chopped green chiles
1 c. frozen peppers and onions,
  thawed and drained

2-1/2 c. shredded Monterey Jack or
  Pepper Jack cheese
1-1/2 doz. eggs, beaten

Garnish: sour cream, salsa

Layer sausage, chiles, pepper mixture and cheese in a greased slow cooker. Repeat layers until all ingredients except eggs and garnish are used, ending with a layer of cheese. Pour eggs over top. Cover and cook on low setting for 7 to 8 hours. Garnish as desired. Serves 10.

Slow-Cooker Hashbrown Casserole

Jessica Robertson, Fishers, IN

32-oz. pkg. frozen shredded
  hashbrowns
1 lb. ground pork sausage,
  browned and drained

1 onion, diced
1 green pepper, diced
1-1/2 c. shredded Cheddar cheese
1 doz. eggs, beaten

1 c. milk
1 t. salt
1 t. pepper

Place 1/3 each of hashbrowns, sausage, onion, green pepper and cheese in a lightly greased slow cooker. Repeat layering 2 more times, ending with cheese. Beat eggs, milk, salt and pepper together in a large bowl; pour over top. Cover and cook on low setting for 10 hours. Serves 8.

Slow-Cooker Hashbrown Casserole

Grandma Rosie's Sausage & Bread Breakfast Pudding

Grandma Rosie's Sausage & Bread Breakfast Pudding

Robin Hill, Rochester, NY

4-1/2 c. Italian bread, cubed and divided
3 Granny Smith apples, peeled, cored and chopped
1 t. cinnamon
1/2 t. allspice
1/4 t. salt
1/4 c. light brown sugar, packed
2 c. milk
1/4 c. maple syrup
16-oz. pkg. ground pork breakfast sausage, browned and divided

Press half the bread cubes into a lightly greased slow cooker; set aside. In a large bowl, combine apples, cinnamon, salt, brown sugar and allspice; mix well. Add milk and maple syrup; stir. Spoon half the apple mixture over bread in slow cooker, pressing down gently. Spoon half the sausage over apple mixture. Layer with remaining bread cubes, sausage and apple mixture. Cover and cook on low setting for 6 hours. Serves 4 to 6.

Biscuits & Sausage Gravy

Erin Brock, Charleston, WV

16-oz. pkg. ground pork breakfast sausage
2 7-1/2-oz. tubes refrigerated biscuits, separated
2 10-3/4 oz. cans cream of mushroom soup

Brown sausage in a skillet over medium heat; drain. Arrange half of the biscuits in the bottom of a greased slow cooker. Layer biscuits with half the sausage and one can of soup. Repeat layers. Cover and cook on low setting for 4 hours, or on high setting for 2 hours. Makes 6 to 8 servings.

Ranch House Breakfast

Rita Morgan, Pueblo, CO

3 qts. boiling water
2 T. salt
2 t. pepper
5 c. steel-cut oats, uncooked
2 lbs. ground beef
2 lbs. ground pork breakfast sausage
2 onions, finely chopped
1/4 c. oil

Combine water, salt and pepper in a slow cooker. Stir in oats; cover and cook on high setting for 1-1/2 hours. In a large bowl, mix together beef, pork, and onions; stir into oat mixture. Cover and cook on low setting for 3 hours, stirring occasionally. Transfer to a 13"x9" baking pan; cool until firm. Turn out onto wax paper and chill for one hour. Cut into thin slices. Heat oil in a large, heavy skillet over medium-high heat. Fry slices until golden. Makes 20 servings.

Country Morning Starter

Christine Camaj, North Salem, NY

16-oz. pkg. ground pork breakfast
  sausage
28-oz. pkg. frozen diced potatoes
16-oz. pkg. shredded mozzarella
  cheese

10 eggs
3/4 c. milk
1 T. biscuit baking mix or pancake
  mix
1/2 t. nutmeg

1/4 t. salt
1/8 t. pepper
Garnish: additional nutmeg
  or pepper to taste

Brown sausage in a skillet over medium heat. Drain; set aside sausage in a bowl. In same skillet, cook potatoes until lightly golden. Transfer potatoes to a slow cooker coated with non-stick vegetable spray. Top potatoes with sausage and cheese; set aside. In a bowl, whisk together remaining ingredients except garnish. Pour egg mixture over cheese layer; stir gently. Sprinkle additional nutmeg or pepper. Cover and cook on low setting for 6 to 8 hours, until eggs are set. Serves 4 to 6.

Breakfast Hot Tots

Jill Ross, Pickerington, OH

14 pork breakfast sausage links,
  sliced
2 c. frozen potato puffs, thawed

2 16-oz. jars chunky salsa
2 c. shredded Monterey Jack
  cheese, divided

1 doz. eggs, beaten
seasoned salt and pepper to taste
Optional: additional salsa

Cook sausage in a skillet over medium heat until browned and no longer pink in the center, about 15 minutes; set aside. Place potato puffs in a lightly greased slow cooker; top with sausage, salsa and one cup cheese. Pour eggs over ingredients in slow cooker; sprinkle with salt and pepper. Cover and cook on high setting for 2-1/2 hours, or until a toothpick inserted in the center tests clean. Top servings with remaining cheese and salsa, if desired. Serves 10.

Country Morning Starter

Championship Cheese Dip

Quick tip

Please the whole gang by having an appetizer party! If your family & friends have different tastes, don't worry about deciding on the perfect main dish...just serve 4 to 5 different appetizers and everyone can choose their favorites.

Championship Cheese Dip

David Wink, Gooseberry Patch

1 lb. ground beef, browned and drained
1/2 lb. spicy pork sausage, browned and drained

32-oz. pkg. pasteurized process cheese spread, cubed
2 10-oz. cans diced tomatoes with green chiles

tortilla chips

Combine all ingredients except chips in a slow cooker; mix well. Cover and cook on low setting for 4 hours, or until the cheese is melted, stirring occasionally. Serve with tortilla chips. Makes 20 to 25 servings.

Nacho Cheese Dip

Sheri Saly, Leesburg, VA

32-oz. pkg. pasteurized process cheese spread, cubed
1-1/2 lbs. ground beef, browned and drained

10-3/4 oz. can cream of mushroom soup
16-oz. jar salsa
tortilla chips

Melt cheese in a microwave-safe bowl, stirring every minute until melted. Combine cheese and remaining ingredients except chips in a slow cooker. Cover and cook on high setting for about one hour. Turn down to low setting to keep dip warm. Serve with tortilla chips. Makes 20 to 25 servings.

Cheesy Mexican Bean Dip

Amy DeLamar Smith, Newport News, VA

31-oz. can refried beans
10-3/4 oz. can nacho cheese soup
1 c. salsa

1 t. salt
1/4 c. green onion, chopped

8-oz. pkg. shredded Cheddar cheese
tortilla chips

In a slow cooker, combine beans, soup, salsa and salt. Cover and cook on low setting for 3-1/2 hours. Sprinkle with green onion and cheese. Cover and cook for an additional 10 minutes, or until cheese is melted. Serve with tortilla chips. Makes 6 to 8 servings.

Extra-Cheesy Mac & Cheese

Valarie Dennard, Palatka, FL

8-oz. pkg. shredded Italian 3-cheese blend

8-oz. pkg. shredded sharp Cheddar cheese

2 eggs, lightly beaten

12-oz. can evaporated milk

1-1/2 c. milk

1 t. salt

3/4 t. dry mustard

1/4 t. cayenne pepper

1/2 t. pepper

2-1/2 c. small shell pasta, uncooked

In a bowl, combine cheeses; set aside. In a separate bowl, whisk together remaining ingredients except pasta. Add pasta and 3 cups cheese mixture; stir well. Spoon pasta mixture into a lightly greased slow cooker. Sprinkle with 3/4 cup cheese mixture; refrigerate remaining mixture. Cover slow cooker and cook on low setting for 4 hours, or until cheese is melted and creamy and pasta is tender. Sprinkle servings evenly with remaining cheese mixture. Serves 6 to 8.

All-Day Mac & Cheese

Laurie Ruell, Rochester, NY

8-oz. pkg. elbow macaroni, uncooked

16-oz. pkg. shredded sharp Cheddar cheese, divided

12-oz. can evaporated milk

1-1/2 c. milk

2 eggs, beaten

1 t. salt

1/2 t. pepper

Cook macaroni according to package directions, just until tender; drain and transfer to a large bowl. Add 3 cups cheese and remaining ingredients. Mix well; spoon into a slow cooker coated with non-stick vegetable spray. Sprinkle with remaining cheese. Cover and cook on low setting for 5 to 6 hours, until firm and edges are golden. Makes 4 to 6 servings.

Zesty Macaroni & Cheese

Jen Licon-Conner, Gooseberry Patch

16-oz. pkg. elbow macaroni, cooked

16-oz. pkg. pasteurized processed cheese, cubed

8-oz. pkg. Pepper Jack cheese, cubed

2 10-3/4 oz. cans Cheddar cheese soup

1 c. onion, minced

1 diced tomato

Place macaroni and cheeses into a slow cooker. Add soup and stir until coated well; add onion and tomato. Cover and cook on low setting for 5 to 6 hours, or on high setting for 2 hours. Stir occasionally. Makes 6 to 8 servings.

Zesty Macaroni & Cheese

Slow-Cooker Veggie Lasagna

Slow-Cooker Veggie Lasagna

Rachel Hodges, Omaha, AR

1-1/2 c. shredded mozzarella cheese
1/2 c. cottage cheese
1/3 c. grated Parmesan cheese
1 egg, beaten
1 t. dried oregano
1/4 t. garlic powder
16-oz. jar marinara sauce
1-1/4 c. zucchini, diced and divided
8 no-boil lasagna noodles
6-oz. pkg. baby spinach, divided
1 c. sliced mushrooms, divided
Optional: fresh basil, chopped

Spray a slow cooker with non-stick vegetable spray. In a bowl, mix together cheeses, egg, oregano and garlic powder. Spread 2 to 3 tablespoons marinara sauce in the bottom of slow cooker. Sprinkle half the zucchini over sauce, top with 1/3 of the cheese mixture. Break 2 noodles into pieces and cover cheese. Spread 2 to 3 tablespoons more sauce over noodles; layer half the spinach and half the mushrooms. Repeat layering, ending with cheese mixture and remaining sauce. Firmly press ingredients into slow cooker. Cover and cook on low setting 4 to 5 hours. Allow lasagna to stand 20 minutes before serving. If desired, garnish with basil. Serves 8.

Quick tip

Quickly dress up a table by filling a glass bowl with seasonal objects…pine cones and ornaments during Winter, dyed eggs in Spring, seashells and sand in Summer and shiny apples during Fall.

Spicy Tortellini & Meatballs

Jennifer Vallimont, Kersey, PA

14-oz. pkg. frozen cooked Italian meatballs, thawed
16-oz. pkg. frozen broccoli, cauliflower and carrot blend, thawed
2 c. cheese tortellini, uncooked
2 10-3/4 oz. cans cream of mushroom soup
2-1/4 c. water
1/2 to 1 t. ground cumin
salt and pepper to taste

Combine meatballs, vegetables and tortellini in a slow cooker. In a large bowl, whisk together soup, water and seasonings. Pour over meatball mixture; stir to combine well. Cover and cook on low setting for 3 to 4 hours. Makes 6 to 8 servings.

Cheesy Spinach Lasagna

Trisha Brady, Knoxville, TN

2 lbs. lean ground beef
2 t. Italian seasoning, divided
2 14-1/2 oz. cans diced tomatoes, divided
2 8-oz. cans tomato sauce, divided
8 c. fresh spinach, torn and divided
3 c. shredded mozzarella cheese, divided
12-oz. pkg. lasagna noodles, uncooked and broken up

Break up uncooked beef and place in a slow cooker sprayed with non-stick vegetable spray. Sprinkle beef with one teaspoon Italian seasoning. Add one can tomatoes with juice and one can tomato sauce; stir gently to combine. Add half of spinach; press down gently. Add one cup cheese and half of uncooked noodles. Repeat layers, ending with cheese on top. Cover and cook on low setting for 8 hours. Makes 6 to 8 servings.

Golden Potatoes & Ham

Marilyn Morel, Keene, NH

6 c. potatoes, peeled and
  sliced
2-1/2 c. cooked ham, cubed
1-1/2 c. shredded Cheddar
  cheese

10-3/4 oz. can cream of
  mushroom soup
1/2 c. evaporated milk

In a slow cooker, layer one-third each of potatoes, ham and cheese. Repeat layers 2 more times. Combine soup and milk and blend until smooth; pour over potato mixture. Cover and cook on low setting for 7 to 8 hours. Makes 4 to 6 servings.

Onion-Topped Potato Casserole

Tina Dammrich, Saint Louis, MO

32-oz. pkg. frozen diced
  potatoes, thawed
2 10-3/4 oz. cans Cheddar
  cheese soup

12-oz. can evaporated milk
salt and pepper to taste
2.8-oz. can French fried
  onions, divided

In a large bowl, combine potatoes, soup, evaporated milk, salt, pepper and half the onions; pour into a greased slow cooker. Cover and cook on low setting for 8 to 9 hours, or on high setting for 4 hours. Sprinkle with remaining onions just before serving. Makes 8 servings.

Ham & Ranch Potatoes

Hope Davenport, Portland, TX

2 lbs. redskin potatoes,
  peeled and quartered
8-oz. pkg. cream cheese,
  softened
1-oz. pkg. buttermilk ranch
  salad dressing mix
10-3/4 oz. can cream of
  potato soup

16-oz. pkg. cooked ham,
  cubed
1 c. shredded Cheddar
  cheese
salt and pepper to taste

Place potatoes in a slow cooker. Combine cream cheese and dressing mix; add soup and mix well. Add cream cheese mixture to slow cooker and mix with potatoes. Cover and cook on low setting for 6-1/2 hours. Stir in ham and top with cheese; add salt and pepper to taste. Cover and cook for another 15 to 30 minutes, until cheese is melted. Serves 6.

Quick tip

For variety, drizzle servings of Onion-Topped Potato Casserole with a bit of chipotle sauce...it adds a great spicy flavor.

Ham & Ranch Potatoes

Mom's Slow-Cooker Mini Reubens

Easy Slow-Cooker Bean Dip

Marni Senner, Long Beach, CA

4 16-oz. cans refried beans
1-lb. pkg. Colby Jack cheese, cubed

1-1/4 oz. pkg. taco seasoning mix
1 bunch green onions, chopped

1 c. sour cream
8-oz. pkg. cream cheese, cubed

Place all ingredients in a slow cooker; stir to mix. Cover and cook on low setting until cheeses melt, about 2 to 3 hours. Stir often. Serves 12.

Mom's Slow-Cooker Mini Reubens

Cheryl Breeden, North Platte, Nebraska

1/4 to 1/2 lb. deli corned beef, chopped
2 6-oz. pkgs. shredded Swiss cheese

8-oz. bottle Thousand Island salad dressing
32-oz. pkg. refrigerated sauerkraut, drained and chopped

Optional: 1 t. caraway seed
1 to 2 loaves party rye bread
Garnish: dill pickle slices

Put all ingredients except party rye and pickles in a slow cooker. Cover and cook on low setting for about 4 hours, or until mixture is hot and cheese is melted. Stir to blend well. To serve, arrange party rye slices and pickles on separate plates around slow cooker. Makes 10 to 12 servings.

Our Favorite Fondue

Jamie Johnson, Columbus, OH

1-1/2 to 2 c. milk
2 8-oz. pkgs. cream cheese, softened

1-1/2 c. grated Parmesan cheese
1/2 t. garlic salt

1 loaf French bread, cubed

In a large saucepan, cook and stir milk and cream cheese over low heat until cream cheese is melted. Stir in Parmesan cheese and garlic salt; cook and stir until heated through. Transfer to a slow cooker; keep warm. Serve with bread cubes. Makes 3-1/2 cups.

Everything's Better with *Cheese*

Twist & Shout Pasta

Barb Sulser, Delaware, OH

2 c. half-and-half
10-3/4 oz. can Cheddar
   cheese soup
1/2 c. butter, melted

16-oz. pkg. shredded
   Cheddar cheese
16-oz. pkg. rotini pasta,
   cooked

In a slow cooker, blend half-and-half, soup and butter until smooth; stir in cheese and pasta. Cover and cook on low setting for 2-1/2 hours, or until cheese is melted. Makes 12 to 15 servings.

Veggie Fettuccine Alfredo

Carol Lytle, Columbus, OH

2 T. butter, softened
2 zucchini, sliced
2 carrots, peeled and thinly
   sliced
1/2 c. sliced mushrooms
1-1/2 c. broccoli, chopped
4 green onions, chopped
3 cloves garlic, minced
1 t. dried basil
1/2 t. salt

1/4 t. pepper
1 c. grated Parmesan
   cheese
16-oz. pkg. fettuccine
   pasta, uncooked
1 c. shredded mozzarella
   cheese
1 c. whipping cream
2 egg yolks, beaten

Grease a slow cooker with butter. Combine vegetables, garlic, seasonings and Parmesan cheese in a slow cooker; stir to mix well. Cover and cook on high setting for 2 hours. Shortly before serving, cook pasta according to package directions; drain and keep warm. Add pasta and remaining ingredients to slow cooker; stir gently to blend. Cover and cook for 10 to 15 minutes more. Serves 4.

Garden-Style Fettuccine

Lisa Hays, Crocker, MO

1 zucchini, sliced 1/4 inch
   thick
1 yellow squash, sliced
   1/4 inch thick
2 carrots, peeled and thinly
   sliced
1-1/2 c. sliced mushrooms
10-oz. pkg. frozen
   broccoli cuts
4 green onions, sliced
1 clove garlic, minced

1/2 t. dried basil
1/4 t. salt
1/2 t. pepper
1 c. grated Parmesan
   cheese
12-oz. pkg. fettuccine
   pasta, cooked
1 c. shredded mozzarella
   cheese
1 c. milk
2 egg yolks, beaten

Place vegetables, seasonings and Parmesan cheese in a slow cooker. Cover and cook on high setting for 2 hours. Add remaining ingredients to slow cooker, stir well. Reduce heat to low setting; cover and cook an additional 14 to 30 minutes. Makes 6 to 8 servings.

Quick tip

Mix up a favorite noodle recipe by substituting different types of pasta. Check out the grocer's for bowties, wagon wheels, shells or alphabet shapes.

Garden-Style Fettuccine

Crustless Mushroom-Swiss Quiche

Quick tip

When shopping for cloth napkins, be sure to pick up an extra one...use it to wrap around a flower pot, pitcher or pail and you'll always have a matching centerpiece.

Quiche Lorraine Bake

Kelly Alderson, Erie, PA

4 slices white bread, toasted and
  crusts trimmed
4 t. butter, softened
2 c. shredded Swiss cheese,
  divided
1/2 lb. cooked ham, diced
6 eggs
1 c. whipping cream or
  half-and-half
1 T. mayonnaise
1/2 t. Dijon mustard
pepper to taste
Optional: 1/8 t. cayenne pepper

Spread toast slices with butter on one side; tear toast into bite-size pieces. Place toast pieces butter-side down in a slow cooker sprayed with non-stick vegetable spray. Layer with half of the cheese, all of the ham and remaining cheese. In a bowl, beat together remaining ingredients; pour over cheese. Cover and cook on high setting for 2 hours, or until eggs are set. Serves 6 to 8.

Crustless Mushroom-Swiss Quiche

Samantha Starks, Madison, WI

4 slices bacon
1 T. olive oil
16-oz. pkg. mushrooms,
  chopped
1/2 c. red pepper, chopped
10-oz. pkg. frozen chopped
  spinach, thawed and very well
  drained
1-1/2 c. shredded Swiss cheese
8 eggs
2 c. half-and-half or milk
2 T. fresh chives, snipped
1/2 t. salt
1/4 t. pepper
1/2 c. biscuit baking mix

In a skillet over medium heat, cook bacon until crisp; drain on paper towels and crumble. Drain skillet; add oil to skillet and heat over medium heat. Sauté mushrooms and red pepper in oil until tender. Stir in spinach and cheese; remove from heat. In a bowl, beat together eggs, half-and-half or milk, chives, salt and pepper. Stir mushroom mixture into egg mixture. Sprinkle with biscuit mix and stir gently. Pour egg mixture into a lightly greased slow cooker; sprinkle bacon on top. Cover and cook on low setting for 4 to 5 hours, or on high setting for 2 to 2-1/2 hours, until a knife tip inserted into the center tests clean. Let stand for 15 to 30 minutes before serving. Makes 6 to 8 servings.

Savory Zucchini Bake

Jo Ann

6 zucchini, sliced 1/2-inch thick
1 t. salt, divided
2 T. olive oil
1 onion, chopped
1 red pepper, chopped
1 clove garlic, minced

1 c. soft bread crumbs
1/3 c. shredded Parmesan cheese
1 t. Italian seasoning
1/4 t. pepper
1 T. butter, diced

Place zucchini in a colander; sprinkle with 1/2 teaspoon salt and let stand for 30 minutes. Rinse well; drain and pat dry. Meanwhile, heat oil in a skillet over medium heat. Sauté onion and red pepper until softened, about 5 minutes. Add garlic; cook and stir for one minute. Remove skillet from heat; add zucchini and mix well. In a bowl, mix bread crumbs, cheese, seasoning, remaining salt and pepper. Transfer half of zucchini mixture to a greased slow cooker. Sprinkle with half of crumb mixture. Repeat layering; dot with butter. Cover and cook for 4 to 5 hours on low setting, until zucchini is tender. Makes 4 to 6 servings.

Mexican Hominy

Mary Stephenson, Grovespring, MO

2 15-1/2 oz. cans yellow hominy, drained
2 15-1/2 oz. cans white hominy, drained
4-oz. can chopped green chiles

8-oz. container sour cream
1 c. shredded Colby cheese
1/2 t. onion powder
1/4 t. garlic powder
salt to taste

Combine all ingredients in a greased slow cooker. Cover and cook on low setting for 2 to 3 hours, until hot and bubbly. Serves 8.

Asparagus & Cheese Hot Dish

Dianna Likens, Powell, OH

1-1/2 to 2 lbs. asparagus, trimmed and sliced
1 egg, beaten
1 c. saltine cracker crumbs
10-3/4 oz. can cream of asparagus soup

10-3/4 oz. can cream of chicken soup
1/4 lb. pasteurized process cheese spread, cubed
2/3 c. slivered almonds

Combine all ingredients in a slow cooker; mix well. Cover and cook on high setting for 3 to 3-1/2 hours, until asparagus is tender. Makes 4 to 6 servings.

Asparagus & Cheese Hot Dish

Eggs with Cheddar & Bacon

Quick tip

There's nothing easier than sprucing up a table with flowers...cluster a small bunch of garden roses in a teapot, add a bouquet of daffodils to an old-fashioned milk bottle or arrange fresh daisies in a watering can. It's so simple!

Eggs with Cheddar & Bacon

Lora Montgomery, Delaware, OH

3 to 4 c. crusty bread, diced
1/2 lb. bacon, crisply cooked,
   crumbled and 1 T. drippings
   reserved

Optional: 2 to 3 c. favorite
   vegetables, chopped
8 eggs, beaten
1/2 c. milk

1 c. shredded Cheddar cheese
salt and pepper to taste

Place bread in a lightly greased slow cooker. If using vegetables, heat reserved drippings in a large skillet over medium heat. Sauté vegetables, tossing to coat. Stir bacon and vegetables into bread. Whisk together eggs and milk in a medium bowl; stir in cheese, salt and pepper. Pour over bread mixture. Cover and cook on low setting for 3 to 3-1/2 hours, until eggs are set. Makes 6 to 8 servings.

Scrambled Eggs Deluxe

Nola Coons, Gooseberry Patch

1/2 lb. bacon, cut into one-inch
   pieces
8-oz. pkg. sliced mushrooms
3 T. butter
16 eggs

1 c. milk
1/2 t. salt
1/4 t. pepper
10-3/4 oz. can cream of mushroom
   soup

2 T. fresh chives, chopped
4 roma tomatoes, chopped and
   divided
8-oz. pkg. shredded Cheddar
   cheese, divided

In a skillet over medium heat, cook bacon until crisp; remove bacon to paper towels. Drain skillet, reserving one tablespoon drippings. Sauté mushrooms in reserved drippings for 4 to 5 minutes, until tender. Set aside mushrooms in a bowl. Wipe out skillet with a paper towel; add butter and melt over medium-low heat. In a large bowl, beat together eggs, milk, salt and pepper. Add egg mixture to skillet; lightly scramble eggs until set but still moist. Stir in soup and chives. Spoon half of egg mixture into a lightly greased slow cooker. Top with half each of mushrooms, tomatoes, cheese and crumbled bacon; repeat layers. Cover and cook on low setting for 30 minutes, or until hot and cheese is melted. May be kept warm on low setting up to 2 hours. Serves 10 to 12.

Cheesy Parmesan Polenta

Jill Burton, Gooseberry Patch

9 c. chicken broth
1/4 c. butter, sliced

1 bay leaf
3 c. instant polenta, uncooked

3 c. grated Parmesan cheese

In a saucepan over medium heat, bring broth, butter and bay leaf to a boil. Gradually whisk in polenta; add cheese and continue whisking until well blended. Transfer to a slow cooker. Cover and cook on low setting for 25 to 30 minutes. Discard bay leaf before serving. Serves 6.

Down-Home Cheese Grits

Stephanie Mayer, Portsmouth, VA

1-1/2 c. stone-ground grits,
  uncooked
6 c. chicken broth or water

2 t. salt
1/4 c. butter, sliced
2 c. whipping cream or whole milk

16-oz. pkg. shredded sharp
  Cheddar cheese
Optional: additional butter

Add grits, broth or water and salt to a lightly greased slow cooker; stir. Cover and cook on low setting for 6 to 8 hours. Shortly before serving time, stir in butter, cream or milk and desired amount of cheese. Cover and let stand several minutes, until cheese is melted. Serve topped with additional butter, if desired. Makes 8 servings.

Savory Corn Spoonbread

Annette Ingram, Grand Rapids, MI

1 c. yellow cornmeal
2 t. baking powder
2 eggs, beaten
1 c. buttermilk

2 T. oil
14-3/4 oz. can creamed corn
1 c. shredded sharp Cheddar
  cheese

Optional: 1 T. canned diced green
  chiles

In a bowl, beat together all ingredients. Pour batter into a greased slow cooker. Cover and cook on low setting for 4 hours, or until a toothpick inserted in the center tests clean. Serve warm. Serves 4 to 6.

Cheesy Parmesan Polenta

🥄🔪🍴 *Quick tip*

Be sure to place warm melted butter on the table for guests to brush over vegetables or rolls. Make a natural butter brush by bundling sprigs of fresh herbs such as thyme, oregano, parsley or rosemary, then bind them together with jute...adds extra flavor too!

Slow-Cooker Mac & Cheese

Macaroni & 4 Cheeses

Ursula Juarez-Wall, Dumfries, VA

3 c. cooked elbow
  macaroni
1 T. margarine, melted
2 c. evaporated milk
3/4 c. shredded Cheddar
  cheese
3/4 c. shredded Monterey
  Jack or Colby Jack cheese
3/4 c. shredded Gruyère or
  Swiss cheese

3/4 c. pasteurized process
  cheese spread, cubed
1/4 c. onion, finely
  chopped
1/4 c. green pepper, finely
  chopped
1 t. seasoned salt
1/4 t. pepper

Combine macaroni and margarine in a lightly greased slow cooker. Add remaining ingredients; mix well. Cover and cook on high setting for 2 to 3 hours, stirring once or twice. Serves 4 to 6.

Macaroni & Cheese

Liz Plotnick-Snay, Gooseberry Patch

1/2 c. butter
1/2 c. all-purpose flour
2 t. salt
4 c. milk
16-oz. pkg. pasteurized
  process cheese spread,
  cubed

16-oz. pkg. elbow
  macaroni, cooked
1/2 t. mustard
  paprika to taste

Melt butter in a saucepan over medium heat; stir in flour and salt. Gradually add milk and stir until thickened. Stir in mustard. Add cheese, stirring until melted. Combine macaroni and cheese sauce in a slow cooker; sprinkle with paprika. Cover and cook on low setting for 4 hours. Makes 8 servings.

Slow-Cooker Mac & Cheese

Paula Schwenk, Pennsdale, PA

8-oz. pkg. elbow macaroni,
  cooked
2 T. oil
12-oz. can evaporated milk
1-1/2 c. milk

3 c. pasteurized process
  cheese spread, shredded
1/4 c. butter, melted
2 T. dried, minced onion

Combine cooked macaroni and oil; toss to coat. Pour into a lightly greased slow cooker; stir in remaining ingredients. Cover and cook on low setting for 3 to 4 hours, stirring occasionally. Serves 4 to 6.

Ham-Stuffed French Rolls

Barbara Fiecoat, Galena, OH

2 c. cooked ham, finely
   chopped
1/2 c. Cheddar cheese,
   diced
1/3 c. mayonnaise
2 T. green onion, minced
1 t. mustard
1 t. sweet pickle relish

Optional: 2 eggs,
   hard-boiled, peeled
   and chopped
Optional: 2 T. black olives,
   chopped
6 large or 8 small
   French rolls

Combine all ingredients except rolls; set aside. Cut tops
or one end off rolls; scoop out most of soft centers. Fill
rolls with ham mixture; replace tops or ends of rolls.
Place filled rolls in a slow cooker. Cover and cook on low
setting for 2 to 3 hours. Makes 6 to 8 sandwiches.

Spoon Bread Florentine

Vickie

10-oz. pkg. frozen chopped
   spinach, thawed and
   drained
6 green onions, sliced
1 red pepper, chopped
5-1/2 oz. pkg. cornbread
   mix

4 eggs, beaten
1/2 c. butter, melted
1 c. cottage cheese
1-1/4 t. seasoned salt

Combine all ingredients in a large bowl; mix well. Spoon
into a lightly greased slow cooker. Cover, with lid slightly
ajar to allow moisture to escape. Cook on low setting for
3 to 4 hours, or on high setting for 1-3/4 to 2 hours, until
edges are golden and a knife tip inserted in center tests
clean. Makes 8 servings.

Easy Chili Rellenos

Betty Kozlowski, Newnan, GA

2 t. butter
7-oz. can whole green
   chiles, drained and cut in
   strips
8-oz. pkg. shredded
   Cheddar cheese
8-oz. pkg. shredded
   Monterey Jack cheese

14-1/2 oz. can stewed
   tomatoes
4 eggs, beaten
2 T. all-purpose flour
3/4 c. evaporated milk

Spread butter in a slow cooker. Layer chiles and cheeses;
add tomatoes. Stir together eggs, flour and milk; pour
into slow cooker. Cover and cook on high setting for 2 to
3 hours. Serves 6.

Quick tip

Have a fun collection of pie birds? Use
them for placecard holders! Just cut out
cardstock, print on names, then nestle them
right in the beaks. So cute!

Spoon Bread Florentine

Ham & Escalloped Potatoes

Simply Delicious Potatoes

Tasha Friesen, Liberal, KS

32-oz. pkg. frozen diced
  potatoes, thawed
26-oz. can cream of
  chicken soup
16-oz. container sour
  cream

8-oz. pkg. shredded sharp
  Cheddar cheese
8-oz. pkg. pasteurized
  process cheese spread,
  diced

Combine all ingredients in a slow cooker; mix well. Cover and cook on high setting for about 2 hours, until hot and bubbly. Makes 10 to 12 servings.

Fantastic Potatoes

Samantha Starks, Madison, WI

10-3/4 oz. can cream of
  mushroom soup with
  roasted garlic
8-oz. container sour cream

1-1/2 c. shredded Colby
  Jack cheese
32-oz. pkg. frozen diced
  potatoes, divided

Combine soup, sour cream and cheese in a medium bowl; mix well. Spread half the potatoes in a slow cooker that has been sprayed with non-stick vegetable spray. Top with half of soup mixture. Layer on remaining potatoes and top with remaining soup mixture. Cover and cook on high setting for 3-1/2 to 4-1/2 hours. Serves 8 to 10.

Ham & Escalloped Potatoes

Judi Candler, Ridgeway, OH

4 slices baked ham
4 potatoes, peeled and
  sliced
1 onion, sliced
10-3/4 oz. can cream of
  mushroom soup

8-oz. pkg. shredded
  Cheddar cheese, divided
Optional: paprika to taste

Layer ham, potatoes, onion and cheese in a slow cooker, reserving 1/2 cup cheese for topping. Pour soup over cheese; sprinkle with paprika, if desired, and cover with 1/2 cup cheese. Cover and cook on low setting for 8 hours, or on high setting for 4 hours. Serves 4 to 6.

Quick tip

Add some sparkle to the table! Wrap inexpensive beaded bracelets around old canning jars. Set a tea light inside each jar or add simple arrangements of flowers. Guests can even take them home as favors.

Bacon & Cheese Breakfast Casserole

Valerie Sholes, Minneapolis, MN

1 T. oil
1 onion, chopped
32-oz. pkg. frozen shredded
  hashbrowns, thawed
1 green pepper, chopped
1/2 lb. bacon, crisply cooked
  and crumbled

8-oz. pkg. shredded Cheddar
  cheese
8-oz. pkg. shredded mozzarella
  cheese
1 doz. eggs
1 c. skim milk
1 T. dried parsley

1 t. dry mustard
2 t. salt
1 t. pepper
Optional: additional shredded
  Cheddar cheese

Heat oil in a skillet over medium heat. Sauté onion in oil until translucent. Stir in hashbrowns and cook until golden. Place half the hashbrown mixture in a lightly greased slow cooker. Top hashbrown mixture with green pepper, bacon, cheeses and remaining hashbrowns; set aside. In a bowl, beat together eggs, milk, parsley, mustard, salt and pepper. Pour egg mixture over cheese in slow cooker. Cover and cook on low setting for 5 to 6 hours, until a knife tip tests clean. Sprinkle a little extra cheese on servings, if desired. Serves 8 to 10.

Sleep-Over Breakfast Strata

Emily Martin, Ontario, Canada

4 c. day-old white bread, cubed
8 eggs
1-1/2 c. milk
1/2 t. salt

1/2 t. pepper
8-oz. pkg. shredded Cheddar
  cheese
8-oz. pkg sliced mushrooms

3/4 lb. bacon, crisply cooked and
  crumbled

Place bread in a 6-quart slow cooker sprayed with a non-stick vegetable spray; set aside. Beat eggs in a large bowl. Whisk in milk, salt and pepper; stir in cheese and mushrooms. Pour egg mixture evenly over bread; set aside. Cook bacon in a skillet over medium heat until crisp; drain, crumble and sprinkle over top. Cover and cook on low setting for 6 to 8 hours, until eggs have set and top is lightly golden. Uncover and let stand for several minutes before serving. Serves 8 to 10.

Sleep-Over Breakfast Strata

Cajun Crockery Breakfast

Cajun Crockery Breakfast

Heather Garthus, Newfolden, MN

32-oz. pkg. frozen diced potatoes
2 c. ground pork breakfast sausage, browned
1 c. onion, finely chopped
1/2 c. green pepper, chopped
1/2 c. mushrooms, chopped
3 c. shredded sharp Cheddar cheese
1 doz. eggs
salt, pepper and Cajun seasoning to taste
1/4 c. milk

Place half the diced potatoes in a slow cooker; top with all of the sausage and half each of the onion, green pepper, mushrooms and cheese. Repeat layering once more, ending with cheese. In a bowl, beat together eggs, seasonings and milk. Pour egg mixture over ingredients in slow cooker. Cover and cook on high setting for 4 to 6 hours, until a toothpick inserted near the center tests clean. Serves 10.

Slow-Cooked Green Eggs & Ham

April Jacobs, Loveland, CO

6 eggs
1/4 c. milk
1/2 c. plain Greek yogurt
1/2 t. dried thyme
1/2 t. onion powder
1/2 t. garlic powder
1/2 t. salt
1/4 t. pepper
1/3 c. mushrooms, diced
1 c. baby spinach
1 c. shredded Pepper Jack cheese
1 c. cooked ham, diced
Optional: grated Parmesan cheese

In a bowl, whisk together eggs, milk, yogurt and seasonings until smooth. Stir in mushrooms, spinach, cheese and ham. Spoon egg mixture into a lightly greased slow cooker. Cover and cook on high setting for 1-1/2 to 2 hours, until eggs are set. Sprinkle servings with Parmesan cheese, if desired. Serves 6.

That's a Gouda Breakfast!

Amy Butcher, Columbus, Georgia

5 baking potatoes, peeled, cooked, shredded and divided
18 links pork breakfast sausage, sliced and divided
2 c. shredded Gouda cheese divided
1/2 c. sun-dried tomatoes packed in oil, drained and thinly sliced
1/3 c. onion, finely chopped
1 doz. eggs
1/2 c. milk
salt and pepper to taste
Garnish: salsa

Place half the potatoes in the bottom of a lightly greased slow cooker. Sprinkle with half the sausage, one cup cheese, sun-dried tomatoes and onion. Top with remaining potatoes and sausage. In a bowl, beat together eggs, milk, salt and pepper; pour over potato mixture. Cover and cook on low setting for 6 to 7 hours, until eggs are set. Top servings with salsa. Serves 6.

Quick side

No time to bake bread for company on their way? Dress up store-bought refrigerated bread sticks in no time. Separate bread stick dough and lay flat; brush with olive oil and sprinkle sesame seeds and snipped parsley over top. Holding ends of bread sticks, twist 2 times; bake as directed.

Broccoli, Cheese & Rice

Kelly Haught, Wellsville, OH

1 c. long-grain rice, cooked
16-oz. jar pasteurized process
   cheese sauce

2 10-3/4 oz. cans cream of chicken
   soup

2 16-oz. pkgs. frozen broccoli,
   thawed

Combine all ingredients in a slow cooker. Cover and cook on low setting for 3 to 4 hours. Makes 6 to 8 servings.

Cheesy Corn for a Crowd

Jennifer Stacy, Hamler, OH

4 15-1/4 oz. cans corn, drained
4 15-oz. cans creamed corn
8-oz. pkg. shredded Cheddar
   cheese

8-oz. pkg. shredded mozzarella
   cheese
2 8-1/2 oz. pkgs. corn muffin mix
4 eggs, beaten

16-oz. container French onion dip

Combine all ingredients and spoon into a lightly greased slow cooker. Cover and cook on high setting for 4-1/2 hours, or on low setting for 9 hours. Serves 15 to 18.

Green Chile Mac & Cheese

Marian Buckley, Fontana, CA

2 c. mostaccioli pasta, uncooked
2 T. buttermilk
8-oz. pkg. pasteurized process
   cheese, cubed

8-oz. pkg. cream cheese, cubed
1 t. Dijon mustard
12-oz. can evaporated milk
1 c. milk

1/2 c. whipping cream
2 10-oz. cans diced tomatoes with
   green chiles

Spray a slow cooker with non-stick vegetable spray. Add uncooked pasta and remaining ingredients except tomatoes. Stir until well combined. Cover and cook on low setting for 4 hours, or until pasta is tender and cheese is bubbly. Shortly before serving time, stir in tomatoes with juice. Cover and cook for several more minutes, until heated through. Makes 6 servings.

Cheesy Corn for a Crowd

Quick side

Turn ordinary cherry tomatoes into party favorites. Cut off the top of each tomato, scoop out the seeds with a small melon baller and turn over to drain on paper towels. Pipe softened cream cheese into hollowed tomatoes and sprinkle fresh dill over top.

Savory Spinach Soufflé

Cheddar Cheese Strata

Tracy McIntire, Delaware, OH

8 slices bread, crusts trimmed
8-oz. pkg. shredded sharp Cheddar cheese
4 eggs

1 c. light cream
1 c. evaporated milk
1 T. dried parsley
1/4 t. salt
Garnish: paprika

Tear bread into bite-size pieces. Alternate layers of bread and cheese in a slow cooker; set aside. Whisk together eggs, cream, evaporated milk, parsley and salt; pour over top. Sprinkle with paprika. Cover and cook on low setting for 3 to 4 hours. Makes 4 to 6 servings.

Easy Cheese Soufflé

Elizabeth Blackstone, Racine, WI

8 slices white bread, crusts trimmed, quartered and divided
8-oz. pkg. shredded Cheddar cheese, divided
4 eggs

1 c. half-and-half or milk
1 c. evaporated milk
1 t. dried parsley
1/4 t. salt
paprika to taste

In a lightly greased slow cooker, layer half each of bread and cheese; repeat layers. In a large bowl, beat together remaining ingredients; pour over top. Cover and cook on low setting for 3 to 4 hours, until set. Serves 4.

Savory Spinach Soufflé

Angela Murphy, Tempe, AZ

2 16-oz pkgs. frozen spinach, thawed and well drained
1/4 c. onion, grated
8-oz. pkg. low-fat cream cheese, softened

1/2 c. mayonnaise
1/2 c. shredded Cheddar cheese
2 eggs, beaten
1/4 t. pepper
1/8 t. nutmeg

In a bowl, mix together spinach and onion; set aside. In a separate bowl, beat together remaining ingredients until well blended; fold into spinach mixture. Spoon into a lightly greased slow cooker. Cover and cook on high setting for 2 to 3 hours, until set. Serves 4 to 6.

Easy Family-Style Corn

Katie Dick, Olathe, KS

2 12-oz pkgs. frozen corn
8-oz. pkg. cream cheese, cubed

1/4 c. butter, cubed
2 T. sugar

1 t. salt
1/2 t. pepper

Spray a slow cooker with non-stick vegetable spray. Add all ingredients; stir to mix. Cover and cook on low setting for 4 hours, stirring halfway through. Makes 8 to 10 servings.

Grandma's Corn

Dixie Dickson, Sachse, TX

8-oz. pkg. cream cheese
1/4 c. butter
32-oz. pkg. frozen corn

1/3 c. sugar or sugar blend for
  baking

Optional: 1 to 3 T. water

Let cream cheese and butter soften in slow cooker on low setting for about 10 minutes. Add corn and sugar or sugar substitute; stir well until corn is coated with cream cheese mixture. Cover and cook on low setting for 3 to 4 hours, stirring occasionally. If corn seems too thick, add water as needed just before serving. Serves 6 to 8.

Corn & Sausage Bake

Debbie Densmore, Tunbridge, VT

1 lb. smoked Polish sausage, diced
2 32-oz. pkgs. frozen corn, thawed
2 8-oz. pkgs. cream cheese, cubed
1/4 c. butter, cubed

8-oz. pkg. shredded extra sharp
  Cheddar cheese
3 T. milk

3 T. water
2 T. sugar
Optional: 1/2 c. onion, chopped

Brown sausage in a skillet over medium heat; drain. Place sausage in a 6-quart slow cooker; add remaining ingredients. Cover and cook on low setting for 4 hours, or on high setting for 2 hours, until heated through and cheeses are melted. Stir before serving. Makes 16 servings.

Easy Family-Style Corn

Quick tip

Have a cupboard full of mismatched dishes and a drawer full of mismatched flatware? A combination of different colors and patterns makes fun settings for the table, so go ahead and mix it up!

Quick tip

When shopping for cloth napkins, be sure to pick up an extra one...use it to wrap around a flower pot, pitcher or pail and you'll always have a matching centerpiece.

Cheesy Crock Potatoes

Cheesy Crock Potatoes

Daphne Mann, Waukesha, WI

24-oz. pkg. frozen shredded
  hashbrowns, thawed
10-3/4 oz. can cream of potato
  soup

16-oz. container ranch dip
1 to 2 c. shredded Cheddar cheese
salt, pepper and garlic powder to
  taste

6-oz. can French fried onions

Combine hashbrowns, soup, dip, cheese and seasonings in a slow cooker. Cover and cook on low setting for 4 to 6 hours, stirring once. Sprinkle with onions before serving. Serves 4 to 6.

Mama's Ranch Potatoes

Lisa Johnson, Hallsville, TX

2 lbs. redskin potatoes, peeled and
  quartered
1-oz. pkg. buttermilk ranch salad
  dressing mix

8-oz. pkg. cream cheese, softened
10-3/4 oz. can cream of potato
  soup

salt and pepper to taste

Place potatoes in a slow cooker. In a small bowl, combine dressing mix and cream cheese; add soup and mix well. Add cream cheese mixture to slow cooker; stir to combine. Cover and cook on low setting for 7 hours, or on high setting for 3-1/2 hours. Before serving, stir to blend. Makes about 6 servings.

Brachiola Stuffed Beef

Joan Brochu, Hardwick, VT

2 lbs. boneless beef round
  steak
1/2 c. seasoned dry bread
  crumbs
1/2 c. grated Parmesan
  cheese
1 T. garlic, minced
1 egg, beaten
1/4 t. pepper
2 eggs, hard-boiled,
  peeled and sieved
32-oz. jar meatless
  spaghetti sauce,
  divided
cooked linguine pasta

Place steak between 2 lengths of wax paper; pound until thin and set aside. Mix together bread crumbs, cheese, garlic, beaten egg, pepper and sieved eggs; spread over steak. Roll up steak and tie at one-inch intervals with kitchen string. Spread one cup spaghetti sauce in the bottom of a slow cooker; set a rack on top. Place rolled-up steak on rack; cover with remaining sauce. Cover and cook on low setting for 6 to 8 hours, until steak is very tender. Slice between strings and serve on hot linguine. Makes 6 servings.

Mock Pierogies

Kelly Ziemba, Port Saint Lucie, FL

1/2 c. butter, melted
1 c. onion, chopped
6 to 7 potatoes, peeled,
  cubed and cooked
16-oz. pkg. shredded
  Cheddar cheese, divided
16-oz. pkg. bowtie pasta,
  cooked

Combine butter and onion in a slow cooker; add potatoes. Sprinkle with half the cheese. Spread pasta on top; sprinkle with remaining cheese. Cover and cook on low setting for 30 to 40 minutes, stirring occasionally. Serves 6 to 8.

Lazy Pierogie Casserole

Kelly Alderson, Erie, PA

8-oz. pkg. bowtie pasta,
  cooked
4 to 6 potatoes, peeled
  and sliced 1/2-inch thick
2 8-oz. pkgs. shredded
  Cheddar cheese
3/4 c. butter, sliced
3/4 c. bacon, crisply
  cooked and crumbled
1 c. onion, finely chopped
salt and pepper to taste

Layer bowties and remaining ingredients in a slow cooker. Cover and cook on low setting for 7 to 8 hours. Stir gently before serving. Makes 4 to 6 servings.

Mock Pierogies

Eggs Italiana

Eggs Italiana

Mia Rossi, Charlotte, NC

1/2 lb. thinly sliced
   provolone cheese,
   divided
10 eggs, beaten
1 c. milk
1/2 t. pepper
1/4 lb. deli sliced prosciutto
   or ham, chopped

1/2 c. roasted red peppers,
   drained and chopped
1/2 c. canned artichokes,
   drained and thinly sliced
1 T. butter, melted

Set aside 3 cheese slices; chop remaining cheese and place in a large bowl. Add eggs, milk and pepper; whisk well. Stir in remaining ingredients except butter. Brush a slow cooker with butter. Pour egg mixture into slow cooker. Cover and cook on low setting for 3 to 3-1/2 hours. Arrange reserved cheese slices on top. Cover and cook an additional 15 minutes, or just until cheese is melted. Serves 6.

Breezy Brunch Florentine

Cathy Hillier, Salt Lake City, UT

1-1/2 c. shredded Colby
   cheese, divided
9-oz. pkg. frozen spinach,
   thawed and drained
1 c. wheat bread, cubed
1 c. sliced mushrooms
1/2 c. green onions, thinly
   sliced

6 eggs
1-1/2 c. milk
1/2 c. whipping cream
1 t. salt
1 t. pepper
1 t. garlic powder

Sprinkle half the cheese into a lightly greased slow cooker. Top cheese with spinach, bread, mushrooms and green onions. In a bowl, beat together eggs, milk, cream and seasonings. Pour egg mixture over ingredients in slow cooker. Sprinkle remaining cheese on top; do not stir. Cover and cook on high setting for 1-1/2 to 2 hours, until a toothpick inserted near the center tests clean. Serves 6 to 8.

Sunrise Hashbrowns

Amy Butcher, Columbus, GA

28-oz. pkg. frozen diced
   potatoes
2 c. cooked ham, cubed
2-oz. jar diced pimentos,
   drained

10-3/4 oz. can Cheddar
   cheese soup
3/4 c. milk
1/4 t. pepper

In a slow cooker, combine potatoes, ham and pimentos. In a bowl, combine soup, milk and pepper; pour over potato mixture. Cover and cook on low setting for 6 to 8 hours. Serves 4.

Quick tip

A wire egg basket makes sharing the extra bounty from your garden so easy...they're strong and roomy. Don't forget to tuck in a few favorite recipes!

Gram's Scalloped Potatoes

Sandy Coffey, Cincinnati, OH

2 c. warm water
1 t. cream of tartar
10 to 12 potatoes, sliced
1 onion, chopped and
    divided
1/2 c. all-purpose flour
2 t. salt, divided
1/2 t. pepper, divided

1/4 c. butter, sliced and
    divided
10-3/4 oz. can cream of
    mushroom soup
10-3/4 oz. cream of celery
    soup
1 c. shredded Cheddar
    cheese

Mix warm water with cream of tartar in a large bowl.
Add potatoes and toss gently; drain. Add half of the
potatoes to a greased slow cooker; sprinkle with half
each of the onion, flour, salt and pepper. Repeat layering;
top with butter and soups. Cover and cook on high
setting for 3 hours, until potatoes are nearly tender.
Top with cheese; cover and cook on high setting for an
additional 30 minutes. Serves 6 to 8.

Quick tip

When garnishing a dish, instead of using
parsley, use your favorite chopped fresh
herb or quartered cherry tomatoes.

Scalloped Corn & Broccoli

Kathy Grashoff, Fort Wayne, IN

16-oz. pkg. frozen chopped
    broccoli
16-oz. pkg. frozen corn
1/4 c. milk
10-3/4 oz. can cream of
    chicken soup

1 c. American cheese,
    shredded
1/2 c. shredded Cheddar
    cheese

Combine all ingredients in a large bowl and spoon into
a slow cooker. Cover and cook on low setting for 5 to
6 hours. Serves 8 to 10.

Smashed Redskin Potatoes

Kay Marone, Des Moines, IA

5 lbs. redskin potatoes,
    quartered
1 T. garlic, minced
3 cubes chicken bouillon
8-oz. container sour cream

8-oz. pkg. cream cheese,
    softened
1/2 c. butter, softened
salt and pepper to taste

Place potatoes, garlic and bouillon in a large saucepan;
cover with water. Bring to a boil; cook just until potatoes
are tender, about 15 minutes. Drain, reserving cooking
liquid. Place potatoes, sour cream and cream cheese in
a large bowl and mash, adding cooking liquid as needed
until desired consistency is reached. Spoon into a slow
cooker; cover and cook on low setting for 2 to 3 hours.
Stir in butter, salt and pepper just before serving.
Serves 10 to 12.

Scalloped Corn & Broccoli

Garlic Smashed Potatoes

Garlic Smashed Potatoes

Nancy Girard, Chesapeake, VA

3 lbs. redskin potatoes, quartered
4 cloves garlic, minced
2 T. olive oil

1 t. salt
1/2 c. water

1/2 c. spreadable cream cheese
  with chives and onions
1/4 to 1/2 c. milk

Place potatoes in a slow cooker. Add garlic, oil, salt and water; mix well to coat potatoes. Cover and cook on high setting for 3-1/2 to 4-1/2 hours, until potatoes are tender. Mash potatoes with a potato masher or fork. Stir in cream cheese until well blended; add enough milk for a soft consistency. Serve immediately, or keep warm for up to 2 hours in slow cooker on low setting. Makes 4 to 6 servings.

Zippy Smashed Potatoes

JoAnn

3 lbs. new redskin potatoes, halved
1/3 c. water
2 T. ranch salad dressing mix

8-oz. container sour cream with
  chives
1/4 c. fresh chives, chopped

1/3 c. half-and-half
1/2 c. shredded Cheddar cheese
salt and pepper to taste

Combine potatoes and water in a slow cooker; stir to coat potatoes well. Cover and cook on low setting for 5 to 6 hours, until potatoes are tender. Mash potatoes with a fork or potato masher; stir in dressing mix, sour cream and chives. Mix well; stir in half-and-half until potatoes reach desired consistency. Sprinkle with cheese and season with salt and pepper to taste. Potatoes may be kept warm, covered, on low setting for about one hour. Serves 8 to 10.

Company Mashed Potatoes

Gloria Kauffmann, Orrville, OH

5 lbs. redskin potatoes, quartered
1 T. garlic, minced, or to taste
3 cubes chicken bouillon

1 to 2 t. salt
8-oz. container sour cream
8-oz. pkg. cream cheese, softened

1/3 c. butter, sliced
salt and pepper to taste

In a saucepan over medium-high heat, cover potatoes with water; add garlic, bouillon and salt. Bring to a boil; cook until potatoes are tender, about 15 to 20 minutes. Drain, reserving cooking water. Mash potatoes with sour cream and cream cheese to desired consistency, adding reserved water as needed. Transfer potato mixture to a slow cooker. Cover and cook on low setting for 2 to 3 hours. Just before serving, stir in butter; season with salt and pepper. Makes 10 to 12 servings.

Delectable Lemon Cheesecake

Cheri Maxwell, Gulf Breeze, FL

1 c. vanilla wafers, crumbled
3 T. butter, melted
2/3 c. plus 1 T. sugar, divided
1-1/2 t. lemon zest, divided
2 8-oz. pkgs. cream cheese, softened
2 eggs
1 T. all-purpose flour
2 T. lemon juice

In a bowl, combine vanilla wafer crumbs, melted butter, one tablespoon sugar and 1/2 teaspoon lemon zest. Pat into a 7" round springform pan; set aside. In a separate bowl, beat together cream cheese and remaining sugar with an electric mixer on medium speed until smooth. Add eggs; beat for 3 minutes. Add flour, lemon juice and remaining lemon zest; continue beating for one minute. Pour filling into crust. Set pan on a trivet in a slow cooker. Cover and cook on high setting for 2-1/2 to 3 hours. Turn off slow cooker; let stand, covered, for one to 2 hours. Remove pan from slow cooker; cool completely before removing sides of pan. Cover and chill until serving time. Serves 8.

Florida Orange Cheesecake

Dana Cunningham, Lafayette, LA

1-1/2 c. reduced-fat cream cheese, softened
1 T. all-purpose flour
1/2 c. sugar
2 T. orange juice
1/2 t. vanilla extract
3 eggs, lightly beaten
1/2 c. non-fat sour cream
1 t. orange zest
1 c. warm water
Optional: orange zest curls

In a large bowl, combine cream cheese, flour, sugar, juice and vanilla. Beat cream cheese mixture with an electric mixer on medium speed until combined; beat in eggs until smooth. Mix in sour cream until smooth; stir in zest. Spoon filling into a lightly greased 1-1/2 quart casserole dish; cover tightly with aluminum foil. Pour warm water into a large slow cooker; set casserole dish in water. Cover and cook on high setting for 2-1/2 hours, or until center of cheesecake is set. Carefully remove casserole dish to a wire rack; uncover and cool cheesecake. When cool, cover and refrigerate for 4 hours. Garnish slices with curls of orange zest, if desired. Serves 8 to 10.

 Quick tip

A piece-of-cake centerpiece! A cake stand does double duty as a simple platform for chunky candles...wrap a ribbon around each pillar for added color and charm.

Lemony Pear Delight

Emma Brown, Saskatchewan, Canada

6 pears, peeled, halved and cored
1 t. lemon zest
2 T. lemon juice

1/3 c. brown sugar, packed
1/4 t. nutmeg
1/2 c. cream cheese, softened

1/4 c. whipping cream
3 T. chopped pecans, toasted
Garnish: crushed sugar cookies

In a bowl, combine pears, lemon zest and juice; toss gently to coat pears. Sprinkle brown sugar and nutmeg over pears; stir. Spoon pear mixture into a slow cooker. Cover and cook on high setting for 1-1/2 to 2 hours, until pears are soft. Spoon pears into serving bowls. Stir cream cheese and whipping cream into juices in slow cooker. Increase heat to high setting and cook, whisking occasionally, until cream cheese is melted. Evenly spoon cream cheese mixture over pears; sprinkle with pecans and crushed sugar cookies. Serves 6 to 8.

Delectable Lemon Cheesecake

White Chocolate-Strawberry Cheesecake

Chocolate & Graham Cracker Cheesecake

Katie Hodges, Bastrop, TX

6 graham crackers, crushed
1/4 c. butter, melted
2 8-oz. pkgs. cream cheese,
  softened

3/4 c. sugar
3 eggs
1 t. vanilla bean paste

3/4 c. semi-sweet chocolate chips,
  melted and slightly cooled
2 to 3 c. water

In a bowl, combine graham cracker crumbs and melted butter; mix until well moistened. Press crumb mixture into an 8" springform pan; set aside. In a separate bowl, beat together cream cheese and sugar with an electric mixer on medium speed until creamy. Add eggs, one at a time and vanilla; mix until well blended, about 3 minutes. Spoon half the batter over crust in pan. Drizzle melted chocolate into remaining batter bowl; mix well. Spoon chocolate batter over batter in pan; swirl with a knife. Set pan on a wire rack or trivet in a slow cooker; pour water into bottom of slow cooker. Cover and cook on high setting for 2 to 3 hours. Transfer cheesecake to a wire rack to cool. Remove cheesecake from pan; cool completely in refrigerator before serving, about an hour. Serves 8 to 10.

White Chocolate-Strawberry Cheesecake

Tina Butler, Royse City, TX

8 graham crackers, crushed
1/4 c. butter, melted
2 8-oz. pkgs. cream cheese,
  softened

3/4 c. sugar
3 eggs
1 t. clear vanilla extract

1 c. white chocolate chips, melted
  and slightly cooled
21-oz. can strawberry pie filling

In a bowl, combine graham cracker crumbs and butter. Mix well and press into an 8" springform pan; set aside. In a separate bowl, beat together cream cheese and sugar with an electric mixer on medium speed until creamy. Beat in eggs, one at a time, and vanilla; mix until well blended. Beat for 3 minutes, until smooth. Stir the melted white chocolate into the cream cheese mixture; spoon over graham cracker crust in pan. Pour one to 2 cups water into a slow cooker. Set pan carefully in water. Cover and cook on high setting for 3 hours, or until center of cheesecake is set. Remove cake to a wire rack to cool; refrigerate for 3 hours before serving. At serving time, spoon pie filling over cake. Serves 8.

INDEX

INDEX

INDEX

INDEX

Soups, Chowders & Chilis

Send us your favorite recipe

...and the memory that makes it special for you!

If we select your recipe for a brand-new **Gooseberry Patch** cookbook, your name will appear right along with it...and you'll receive a FREE copy of the book!

Submit your recipe on our website at
www.gooseberrypatch.com/sharearecipe or mail to:
Gooseberry Patch, PO Box 812, Columbus, OH 43216

*Please include the number of servings and all other necessary information.

Have a taste for more?

Visit www.gooseberrypatch.com to join our Circle of Friends!
- Free recipes, tips and ideas plus a complete cookbook index
- Get special email offers and our monthly eLetter delivered to your inbox